Mobilizing the U.S. Latinx Vote

This book examines the politics involved in the mobilization of the Latinx vote in America. Delving into the questions of race and identity formation in conjunction with the role of communication media, the author discusses the implications for Latinx voters and their place in the American political and racial system.

Utilizing an in-depth study of the mobilizing efforts of national Latinx groups, along with a rigorous analysis of online media, news media, and electoral results, this book discusses:

- How the old notions of white and black America clash with the growing focus on Latinos
- How political organizers develop and use messages of racial solidarity to motivate people, what technologies are at their disposal, and what their use means
- How the study of new media is vital to exploring race in the 21st century, and why communication cannot ignore the racial legacies of the 20th century

Theoretically located in between the fields of communication and racial/ethnic studies, this book will be of great relevance to scholars and students working in the field of communication studies, political communication, Latinx studies, and sociology.

Arthur D. Soto-Vásquez, PhD, is an Assistant Professor of Communication at Texas A&M International University. He studies the relationship between digital media, popular culture, and identity making. He has previously published award-winning research on digital privacy in U.S. presidential campaigns and on presidential rhetoric regarding Latinxs in the United States. He is from El Paso, Texas.

Routledge Focus on Digital Media and Culture

The *Serial* Podcast and Storytelling in the Digital Age
Edited by Ellen McCracken

Media Piracy in the Cultural Economy
Intellectual Property and Labor Under Neoliberal Restructuring
Gavin Mueller

Mobilizing the U.S. Latinx Vote
Media, Identity, and Politics
Arthur D. Soto-Vásquez

Mobilizing the U.S. Latinx Vote
Media, Identity, and Politics

Arthur D. Soto-Vásquez

Routledge
Taylor & Francis Group

LONDON AND NEW YORK

First published 2020 by Routledge

2 Park Square, Milton Park, Abingdon, Oxon OX14 4RN

605 Third Avenue, New York, NY 10017

Routledge is an imprint of the Taylor & Francis Group, an informa business

First issud in paperback 2021

Publisher's Note

The publisher has gone to great lengths to ensure the quality of this reprint but points out that some imperfections in the original copies may be apparent.

Library of Congress Cataloging-in-Publication Data
A catalog record has been requested for this book

ISBN: 978-0-367-41842-7 (hbk)
ISBN: 978-1-03-217530-0 (pbk)
DOI: 10.4324/9780367816506

Typeset in Times New Roman
by codeMantra

Contents

List of tables   vii
Preface   viii

1 **Introduction: dreams of a united Latinx polity**   1
   Cultural and political change meets Latinxs 2
   Introducing the mediation of U.S. Latinx identity 5
   Methodology 8
   Outline of chapters 12

2 **The mediation of Latinx identity before the Internet**   16
   A note on terminology 17
   Contextualizing the political and economic moment 18
   Racial formation theory applied 19
   Minimization of difference 22
   Denationalization 25
   Racialization 29

3 **New media and U.S. Latinx identity**   35
   Naming in a networked society 38
   The "New Latino" and online expression 40
   Navigating U.S. politics as a Latinx 43

4 **Political mobilization in the post-modern digital era**   49
   Digital politics—tools, opportunities, and
     vulnerabilities 49
   Campaigns and political advertising online 52
   Voters as audience-identity constructions 54
   Post-modern identity and politics 57
   Towards a "New Latino" hybrid 59

5   **The professional political class of U.S. Latinxs**   63
    Minimization of difference 65
    Denationalization 69
    Racialization 73
    Networked Latinx identity formation 77

6   **Latinx presentation, digital representation**   79
    Platforms and messages 82
    The end of DACA 87
    The shutdown 89
    The 2018 Texas Democratic primary 92
    New tools, old practices? 94

7   **Media coverage of the 2018 midterms**   97
    How the media talked about Latinx voters 98
    Minimization of difference 99
    Denationalization 101
    Racialization 103
    Telling the Latinx story 105

8   **Conclusion**   109
    Findings summarized 111
    Contributions summarized 114
    Limitations of the study 115
    Recommendations 117
    Future directions 121

    Index   125

Tables

5.1	Prototypical narratives of Mexican American success	75
6.1	Tweets collected by time period	82
7.1	Data by news medium	98
7.2	Themes of U.S. Latinx identity making in news coverage	99
7.3	Counter themes of U.S. Latinx identity making in news coverage	99

Preface

Election night in Washington, D.C.

On the evening of November 8, 2016, I departed my apartment in Washington, D.C., to watch the election results downtown. The event was organized by Voto Latino, a national Latinx advocacy organization focused on increasing Latinx civic engagement. Like many events in the nation's capital organized by political groups, I secured my invitation through a friend. As a graduate student, I was happy to have some free food and drink. Like many in the room, I expected the Democratic candidate, Hillary Clinton, to win easily that night. And like many others across the country, we ended the evening confused about what had just happened.

In the days leading up to the election, there was exciting news coming out of Arizona and Florida regarding early voting. Latinx turnout looked massive and unprecedented. Lines at polling stations in Phoenix and Orlando stretched around the block. News pundits had speculated that the nativist rhetoric of the Republican nominee, Donald Trump, would drive huge increases in Latinx turnout. In Florida, the recent immigration of Puerto Ricans from the economically troubled island to the Interstate-4 corridor (Tampa Bay and Orlando) was discussed as a new factor in the electoral calculus. In Arizona, Latinx voters in Maricopa County had the chance to vote out hardline anti-immigrant sheriff Joe Arpaio.

Early voting results in other states with lots of Latinx voters also looked promising in the days leading up to the election. In Texas, there were long lines at polling places in counties like Harris and Bexar. Harris and Bexar have huge populations of Mexicans and Mexican Americans in Houston and San Antonio, respectively. All these news items, which I manically devoured leading up to election day, gave me an extra spring in my step as I walked to my Metro stop in D.C.

I was also enthused by the larger potential political results: another Democratic president and the flipping of some previously red states, like Arizona. And I was excited by the implications for my academic research.

Throughout the 2010s, there was general excitement around the changing demographics of the United States. Many believed that the growing share of Latinx voters could produce a permanent Democratic majority. I personally have been researching issues around Latinx politics since 2009. Some of my projects focused on the rhetorical framing of Latinxs in politics, national Latinx political organizations, and online social movements. I figured that the 2016 election would conform to my preconceived notions of the rise of Latinx voters and my work would have a nicely tied bow on top of it.

As I walked to the Metro station streaming live video from Twitter on my mobile phone, everything looked good. Clinton was still expected to win. I boarded the Metro car and, without data access, let my mind wander as I looked through the window into the dark underground tunnel. I do not remember what I was thinking about. For dramatic purposes, I wish I'd had more profound thoughts, but I'll have to disappoint readers here. I felt confident enough about the outcome of the election to not be bothered by too much anxiety.

The environment inside the venue immediately shook my confidence, as I could feel the nervousness of the mostly Latinx attendees. While I found some appetizers and a drink, my friend fired off some concerning factoids to me. Results in Kentucky, the first state to report results, showed a trend of voters who had voted for Barack Obama in 2012 defecting toward Trump.

Readers know the end of the story. As results rolled in, the crowd at the Voto Latino event began to talk and move with a quick, nervous unease. Most gazed in disbelief at their phones, desperately refreshing their social media feeds for more information. A friend at my table kept peeking in despair at the *New York Times* probability dial, which slowly ticked toward predicating Trump's win. Others in the room began trading business cards in anticipation of whatever strange circumstances and shifting alliances might come in the months ahead.

Scenes of disbelief and confusion like what I described will probably fill hundreds of books and dissertations over the next few years. The 2016 election scrambled so many expectations across so many fields of study. On a train ride to Philadelphia the next day, I reflected on my own intellectual journey studying Latinx politics. I realized that my work would have to take a whole new direction in the Trump era. Somewhere along the way, I vaguely resolved to understand how

Latinxs in the United States would respond to this new political environment.

What follows is my own attempt to understand the recent history of Latinx politics online in the United States. My training as a scholar of communication studies informs how the decisions and strategies I observed over a year are interpreted through a system of analysis drawn from communication theory. I also rely on the critical Latinx studies perspective to fill in the gaps missing in mainstream political communication theory. At the same time, I do not come to this project as a dispassionate observer. I am very much invested in the future of Latinxs in the United States. Since 2010, I have been interested in this topic intellectually, but as a Latinx person, I am also a subject of this political process.

I also enjoy many social privileges as a researcher. I am associated with prestigious academic institutions and I deploy social capital to move within the spaces I research. I can easily code-switch to the professionalized communication styles of elite Latinx actors. The performance of myself such as how I appear, dress, and speak, all make me a perfect insider to study this phenomenon. No doubt I belong in the spaces I enter, and I can seamlessly move in and out. I state my positionality as a researcher here not to argue that others cannot research a topic they are not personally perfectly suited for. Neither do I suggest my knowledge is more authentic or valid than others. Simply, I believe all researchers should be cognizant of where they come from when doing field research and for readers to have a sense of who I am at the outset of this book.

This book is a culmination of research conducted between 2017 and 2019, the first months of the Trump presidency leading up to and including the midterms elections. It is not exactly what I imagined doing when I first started researching this topic, but it is way more exciting.

1 Introduction

Dreams of a united Latinx polity

Leading up to the 2016 election, there was a hope among Democrats that the inflammatory rhetoric toward immigrants of the Republican candidate for president, Donald Trump, would inspire Latinx voters to the polls and deliver victory. While the election outcome they hoped for did not happen, Latinx voters began to show their power at the polls. Even in Texas, a GOP stronghold since the 1980s, Hillary Clinton improved on Barack Obama's vote total by eight million votes—an accomplishment credited to increased Latinx participation.

In the aftermath of the 2016 election, there was also a small but important controversy over the purported 20% or so of Latinxs who, according to exit polls, voted for Trump. A similar pattern emerged in exit polls from Texas in the 2018 midterms. This flummoxed the national press and others: how could this many Latinxs vote for someone so oppositional to immigrants? More recent electoral studies have complicated those exit poll results, but nonetheless the controversy demonstrates the challenges in analyzing the Latinx electorate as a singular, fixed political entity.

The intense focus on Latinx voters is part of a surge of attention among political leaders, researchers, media organizations, and countless pundits regarding the changing demographics of the nation and the emergence of Latinxs (Taylor, Gonzalez-Barrera, Passel, Lopez, 2012). As a demographic category, Latinxs have grown as a proportion of the populace dramatically in recent history. The political discourse of demographic change deserves much more critical attention. Both major political parties in the United States, Democrats and Republicans, have devoted significant time and energy to capturing and engaging Latinxs in their coalitions. Following the 2012 elections, party documents from the GOP highlighted the need to pursue certain policy reforms, such as immigration reform and reducing the volume of nativist rhetoric among the party's most conservative members to appeal to Latinxs. Following the 2014 elections, party documents from the Democrats revealed a similar strategy of further appealing to Latinxs, especially Latinas, to expand their multiethnic coalition. The 2016 and 2018 elections showed continued outreach toward Latinx communities by multiple campaigns. The last two decades have also seen a rise in anti-immigrant rhetoric and anti-Latinx racism (Chavez, 2013), yet some feel a budding optimism that Latinxs will rejuvenate and transform U.S. politics (Barreto, Segura, 2014). This omnipresent demographic optimism has been repeated continually in national Latinx conferences since at least 2014. A version of the phrase "once Latinx begin to show up to the polls, everything will be okay" has been a common refrain at conferences I've attended since at least 2012.

In this book, I argue that this surge of attention holds a key implication for how we think about race, communication, media, and politics. The process of organizing and mobilizing Latinxs into voting constituencies taps into powerful racial scripts and produces a new Latinx identity. This Latinx identity is highly commodified and acts more like a brand than a racial identity. I argue that this is symptomatic of the political and cultural times we live in, the people behind Latinx political organizing, and the digital tools used to communicate to Latinx audiences.

Cultural and political change meets Latinxs

Corporations and other commercial interests have taken notice of the emerging Hispanic market in the United States and seek to capture the potentially immense buying power of over 50 million people. For marketers, Latinx attention and consumption are hot commodities waiting to be captured. As a result, a $5-billion marketing industry has emerged, with growth outpacing general audience marketing (Dávila, 2012). Media organizations are also becoming more aware of the commercial implications of a growing Latinx audience. Univision launched a new bilingual channel aimed at the millennial demographic called Fusion, and multiple online media platforms, such as *Flama*, *MiTú*, and *Pero Like*, began gaining prominence in the late 2010s. Marketing and bilingual media are targeted toward the emerging concept of the "new Latinx," a cosmopolitan, educated, and Americanized Latinx (Chavez, 2013)—a concept I'll return to later in the book.

The Latinx population in the United States is also a young one. The average age of a white person in the United States is 56. The median age of a Latinx person is 19 years (Patten, 2016). The youth of the U.S. Latinx population inspires many groups to organize and turn out their vote. It also excites sponsoring advertisers who see potential in Latinx purchasing power and the chance to capture young consumers in their prime habit-forming years.

The rhetorical construction of U.S. Latinxs as a new and growing population obfuscates the long and complicated history Latinxs have had with the nation state. Latinxs of many different origins have lived and democratically participated in the United States for decades. Mexicans living in the Southwest suddenly became U.S. citizens following the signing of the Treaty of Guadalupe Hidalgo in 1848 after the United States invaded Mexico. Puerto Ricans were U.S. citizens for most of the 20th century after previously being colonial subjects. However, neither enjoyed full citizenship in practice. Immigrant groups from the Caribbean, Central America, and beyond settled throughout the country many years before the post-NAFTA wave of immigration.

Despite the long history of Latinxs in the United States, the recent increase in interest is especially noteworthy. It deserves attention not because "Latinxs have arrived" but because of the political and economic capital that now is at stake. U.S. Latinxs are being viewed as both a viable electoral community and a powerful marketable entity. This attention can be exciting, but it also needs serious critical engagement and unpacking. The effort to mobilize Latinx voters in the United States has been a decades-long project, intensifying in scale and urgency in the 2010s. One of the factors that led to the intensification was the recognition based on demographic data that Latinxs were becoming a larger portion of the population. There was also a recognition of political constituencies shifting toward ethnic party identification in the 2008 election, with Republicans representing the interests of whites (especially men) and the Democrats representing those of everyone else, but especially ethnic minorities and women (Abramowitz, 2010).

Multiple stakeholders from civic organizations, advocacy groups, political parties, and media organizations have launched various efforts to mobilize Latinxs. Latinx youth mobilization, voter registration, and promulgating voting information have been some of the specific campaigns, yet a common thread has been a heavy focus on digital and online organization. Using digital platforms such as websites, social media, mobile applications, and digitally mediated meetups, organizations are, as a byproduct, making claims about the U.S. Latinx community.

U.S. Latinx advocacy groups used to generally be legacy intuitions, such as the League of United Latin American Citizens (LULAC) and the National Council of La Raza (now called UnidosUS), which advocated for civil rights in Latinx communities. Newer, digital-first groups such as Voto Latino and United We Dream are now in this group of organizations. I use the term "digital first" to delineate a difference between groups founded in the pre-Internet era, and those founded after that primarily organize their constituencies online. As Karpf (2012) argues in *The MoveOn Effect*, we can roughly draw a line between how advocacy organizations in the United States related to their audiences before and after 2008. The line is the transition from mail- or phone-based membership-sustaining organizations to short-term contingent, Internet-based memberships. I use the term *hybrid media environment* (Chadwick, 2013) in my research questions to refer to this process which mixes old and new media.

We also must recognize that in the 2010s, especially the latter half of the decade, we have seen racial difference and strife bubble up into mainstream issues. Perhaps the first incident in my own memory was the failed immigration reforms of 2007. I was a freshman in high school in El Paso, Texas. I really did not understand the full details of the proposed policy, but I did feel that what was happening was an attack on my personhood. I ended up participating in a walkout to protest the policy. Afterward, the election of Barack Obama potentially represented a break from racial politics and a post-racial era for some. This was quickly proven unrealistic with various controversies, such as the birther movement and the reaction to the Black Lives Matter movement. For Latinxs, issues around immigration persisted; activists I talked to were always quick to point out that President Obama deported more undocumented immigrants than any other president. All of this is to say that the communications process studied in this book occurred in a highly racialized time.

These trends led to the current moment. The United States is in the midst of a demographic change unseen since the late 19th century. The racial system was designed for a black/white population in the pre-industrial era. So, what will be the racial order of our current economic system? Our post-industrial, information-based economy is highly mediated and hybridic. From that perspective, what role does the Internet and digital media play in shaping Latinx identity? And to that point, who are the organizations and actors in the U.S. Latinx project, and what role do they play? It is clear that this new market of voters and consumers is attractive to political and corporate interests. These larger questions, debates, and tensions set the stage for this book's focus on identity building in the current political and technological moment.

Introducing the mediation of U.S. Latinx identity

In Soto-Vásquez (2018), I analyzed how U.S. presidents since the Kennedy administration have used different terms to address Latinx subjects. The results of the research suggest that presidents use the practice of naming Latinx subjects to further their own political agendas and reinforce economic and foreign policy goals. For example, the administration of John F. Kennedy used expressions such as "Americans of Mexican extraction" to describe successful Latinxs in society. Kennedy did this to demonstrate the superiority of the American way of life, democracy, and market capitalism compared to Soviet-styled communism. The Kennedy administration used terminology about Latinxs, and eventually nominated the first Mexican American ambassador, to prevent Soviet ideology from gaining a foothold in Latin America. It is less useful to treat Latinx identity as a fixed category where someone either is or is not Latinx. Instead, this book, following the lead of many prominent Latinx scholars, makes the argument that Latinx identity is closer to a black box of abstraction. The flexibility of the term lends itself to use by political actors pursuing vastly divergent political agendas.

Introducing digital technologies into the mix also complicates Latinx identity. On the Internet, there is the tendency to both entrench racial and ethnic identity and deconstruct it. For example, in late 2017, two immigration-related events occurred. First, there was the campaign to advocate legislative action on the Deferred Action for Childhood Arrivals (DACA)[1] after the Trump administration ended the regulation. Second, the Trump administration also ended Temporary Protected Status (TPS)[2] for immigrants of several nationalities, including many Central Americans. The second event was much less prominent in the mainstream news.

Upon closer examination, the response to these two events demonstrated the tendency of the Internet to entrench and complicate Latinx identity. Most of the organizations I study in this book heavily pushed for Congress to act on DACA in late 2017 and early 2018. They often used rhetoric aimed to galvanize all Latinxs, not just those affected by the repeal, to become involved by calling their congressional representatives. In effect, the message was "all Latinxs need to stand up to protect Dreamers." Here was the tendency for organizations online to reinforce a broad notion of Latinx identity to advance a specific goal.

The ending of TPS was emphasized less among the organizations I studied. I did find a small but prominent group of Central American activists online arguing that the relative erasure of TPS compared to

DACA was a serious oversight by national Latinx figures. In their own rhetoric, they challenged the notion of Latinx unity. They argued that the hegemonic dominance of Mexican Americans in Latinx politics often ended up reflecting the interests of Mexican Americans, just with a veneer of a broader ethnic label. Here was the other tendency of the Internet—providing spaces online for marginalized subjects to come together and critique the construction of Latinx identity.

Each of these tendencies will emerge consistently throughout the book in my analysis of the interviews, events, digital products, and news items I collected throughout the past three years. Guiding my analysis is the idea that Latinx identity in the United States is often constructed as pan-ethnic. What does this mean? Multiple ethnic identities, with ancestry traced throughout Latin America, are folded into a simple category for consumption. I have referred to this process as an abstraction of ethnic identity, and others (accurately) refer to it as a process of contemporary racialization. This conversation about racialization will be discussed more in depth in Chapter 2.

So how exactly does this process work? Latinx abstract pan-ethnicism refers to the subversion of the ethnic, racial, and national differences between communities throughout Latin America. These differences are erased and replaced with a simple and corporate U.S. Latinx label. Several prominent Latinx scholars have offered their takes on this process. These include perspectives on how Spanish-language news media (Rodriguez, 1999), ethnic marketing (Dávila, 2012), advocacy groups (Beltran, 2010), and even the creation of the term *Hispanic* (Mora, 2014) have shaped Latinx identity.

From each of these perspectives, I have synthesized a generalized process of how U.S. Latinx identity is formed for this book. There are generally three distinct processes of Latinx identity making: the minimization of difference, denationalization, and racialization (Soto-Vásquez, 2018). The minimization of difference, which I will sometimes refer to as homogenization, is erasing the many ethnic, racial, class, geographic, and other differences of people with Latin American ancestry. Denationalization works similarly; the unique national identities and histories of immigrant groups are all subsumed into the Latinx identity machine and Americanization is encouraged. Finally, racialization works by articulating Latinx identity into a separate and distinct category from white and black people. These three processes also happen interpendently; let me show how in a hypothetical example.

Two immigrants come from Mexico. One is a wealthy young woman from Mexico City. She is proud to be of European descent, and her features are closer to the Eurocentric ideal of beauty in the West. Because of her wealth and social status, she can easily move between Mexico, the United States, and the rest of the world. She is multilingual and cosmopolitan. The class she represents in Mexico tends to be conservative, and dismissive of the concerns of the poor. The second immigrant also comes from Mexico but from a southern state called Oaxaca. Her local community has suffered since the enactment of NAFTA and the destruction of subsistence farming via an influx of crops into Mexico. Many of her community members have been forced to migrate either to northern Mexico to work in maquiladoras or to the United States. Most do not have the means to cross legally and thus become enmeshed in a draconian immigration system. She has the features of a mestizo person, a mix of indigenous and other ancestries.

Now imagine if both subjects came to the United States. Somehow these two women, with vastly different backgrounds and class status, are both Latina. This abstraction exists despite the many fissures and tensions that would occur between the two women in Mexico. The wealthy woman's class compatriots welcomed the enactment of NAFTA and the neo-liberalization of Mexico's economy. NAFTA eliminated the longtime legal practice of communally held lands and devastated the rural poor, especially in the south. There is also likely a strong element of colorism present.

Now flash forward 20 years. Both women are raising families in the United States. Our wealthy subject has done quite well and her family can frequently travel. The children attend private schools and are multilingual. Our impoverished woman has raised children while constantly fearing immigration raids. Her kids are also multilingual but have been told that their ability to succeed in the United States is dependent upon a good education and "leaving the neighborhood." The wealthy kids have a notion of culture and citizenship that is entirely different. Their world is cosmopolitan and interconnected. Despite the differences, both families are addressed as Latinx subjects. They are asked to enact their U.S. citizenship and pursue the "American dream." They are both invited to join Latinx groups at their colleges and within their professional trades. Much of the difference that exists on the inside is erased by media and social influence on the outside.

Rodriguez, for example, argues cogently,

> the production and dissemination of the notion of Latinx pan-ethnicity (the core of which is the elimination of national origin and racial differences) in Hispanic marketing and commercial

representation since 1980 has erased the distinct immigration histories as well as the adaptation and settlement patterns of the three principal Latin American immigrant groups in the United States.

(22)

Her quote touches upon two of these processes. The minimization of difference happens when different immigrant histories are glazed over—think back to the different reactions to DACA and TPS ending. Denationalization also occurs when nationalities are melded together into the abstract Latinx label.

In another example, we can think broadly about how in the national political discourse immigration is tied to Latinx politics. Given the uneven developments of transnational relations between Latin American countries and the United States, the tying of immigration to Latinx issues and the Latinx body politic is an exemplar of the erasing of unique immigration histories in pan-ethnic discourse. I raise immigration not to dispute that there is perhaps some sense of solidarity between national origin groups but to demonstrate how national political discourse simplifies and essentializes Latinx identity for expediency.

Returning to the scholars mentioned earlier, a common thread is the focus they place on the role of media to communicate Latinx identity. Rodriguez looks at Spanish-language news placing Latinxs in everyday life. Dávila focuses on how commercials for Coca-Cola and Goya were produced and marketed to Spanish-speaking audiences. Yet for me, the unresolved question is how the process of Latinx identity formation happens in online spaces. As mentioned earlier, social media online allows for two contradictory tendencies: to entrench racialization and to challenge it. This is a much larger question for scholars to tackle, since it occurs as a result of many more facets of human- and computer-mediated communication than this book is focused on. However, my hope is that this work can provide both a framework for understanding the process of Latinx identity creation in the digital era and a prototype study of how to conduct the research.

Methodology

The overall methodological approach of this book is qualitative and is about understanding the meaning of various identity formation practices and communication strategies related to the political mobilization of U.S. Latinxs. I am charting a recent history of the terminology and politics of being Latinx in the United States. It is also relational in the sense that my research focused on subjects in relation to their organizations, their ties to center-left political networks, and their fluency in digital Latinx politics. My work here situates the subjects in larger historical debates and within networks where Latinx identity is contested and produced. I utilized a variety of methods to collect data including a series of informal conversational interviews and semi-structured, standardized expert interviews over the course of late 2017 and early 2018. Informal conversational interviews are typically unplanned and unanticipated interactions with research subjects in the field; they often occur naturally when the researcher is doing fieldwork. The primary source of interview data is the semi-structured, standardized expert interviews. These semi-structured, standardized expert interviews were conducted face to face. Interviews typically lasted 30–45 minutes and took place in office settings and semiformal spaces, such as coffee shops.

I was able to interview several representatives of Voto Latino, LULAC, and the Congressional Hispanic Caucus. Representatives from UnidosUS did not respond to my request for an interview. All interview subjects' official titles were either director or vice president. I chose to talk to elite subjects within the organization for a specific reason. I wanted to gain access to decision makers within an organization. In many cases, I also used LinkedIn and other data sources to complement the data I collected.

I also studied the role of national conventions as sites where actors come together to strategize, formalize priorities, test out rhetoric, and network. To answer this question, I conducted ethnographic field observations of five national Latinx conferences over the summer and fall of 2017. These conferences included the annual conventions of the National Association of Latinx Elected and Appointed Officials (NALEO) in Dallas, TX; the League of United Latin American Citizens (LULAC) in San Antonio, TX; the National Council of La Raza (NCLR, now UnidosUS) in Phoenix, AZ; and Voto Latino in Austin, TX.

Qualitative field research "enables researchers to observe social life in its natural habitat," which often cannot be captured by quantitative methods (295). Participant observation is especially useful for documenting social situations of smaller or niche groups of interests (Lofland, Snow, Anderson, Lofland, 2009). In her study of the emerging Mexican American middle class, Vallejo (2012) used a similar method of participant observation in addition to in-depth interviews.

I relied primarily on participant observation, which is "the systematic description of events, behaviors, and artifacts in the social setting chosen for study" (Marshall, Rossman, 2016, 79). Kawulich (2005, 81) adds:

> The process of conducting this type of field work involves gaining entry into the community, selecting gatekeepers and key informants, participating in as many different activities as are allowable by the community members, clarifying one's findings through member checks, formal interviews, and informal conversations, and keeping organized, structured field notes to facilitate the development of a narrative that explains various cultural aspects to the reader.

Attending the full annual conferences, from the opening plenaries to the closing sessions, allowed for observation of multiple activities. At most conferences, I attended sessions relevant to my research question on voter mobilization and identity. Some conferences had panels on digital tech and social media skills, which I also attended.

The conferences conveyed messages through professional speakers and politicians. As a result, I usually played an observer role. However, in between sessions and during socials, I participated in the conference with other attendees. In some cases, the observer role was more complicated, as the divide between speakers and participants was less clear. There, I played more of a participant role, which meant interacting with students and facilitators. However, during work sessions, I mostly stood or sat in the back of the room and observed. In either case, my own presentation as an educated Latinx male did not make me an obvious outsider.

Collecting participant observation data at the national and local levels included several components, such as paying attention; shifting from a "wide" to a "narrow" angle perspective; and focusing on a single person, activity, or interaction and then returning to a view of the overall situation (Freebody, 2002). In both cases, I took extensive field notes on the conferences and collected physical and digital artifacts (brochures, conference websites, video recaps, etc.). By the end of my observations, I had 64 pages of handwritten notes.

I also studied online communication products as units of analysis; I did not conduct a comprehensive analysis of all media created by Latinx organizations in the past few months. I was inspired by the approach of Bruns and Brugess (2012) in selecting a timeframe around major news events to study the role of social media. I looked at news events that impacted U.S. Latinxs and then conducted a close reading of the media texts created in reaction to the events by the organizations I studied. Rather than breadth and generalizability of analysis, I focus here on in-depth analysis of media texts.

I selected three moments related to Latinx issues since the beginning of the Trump administration: the announcement by President Trump in late 2017 that he would end DACA; the short federal government shutdown in early 2018, which partly occurred over immigration issues; and the 2018 primary elections in Texas. In each case, I utilized a two-week time frame to collect texts before and after the event. I utilized the twitter public search API to collect tweets and then saved them in a file.

Texts were drawn from a variety of sources. Instead of selecting communications from one platform over another (for example, tweets over emails), I collected from a wide range of sources. These include social postings from Facebook and Twitter, email communications, and press releases. Once the sample was constituted, I conducted a qualitative content analysis. Qualitative content analysis is a kind of textual analysis. According to Frey, Botan, and Kreps (2007), textual analysis is used to describe the content, structure, and functions of the messages contained in culturally mediated texts. The process of analysis outlined by Bernard and Ryan (1998) is followed here: (1) texts were closely scrutinized, (2) preliminary themes were identified, (3) overarching structures were conceptualized, and (4) theoretical models were constructed. In practical terms, I conducted a close reading of each communication once and then wrote down initial notes. Later, I returned to the sample and began highlighting commonalities, deviances, absences—essentially anything that piqued interest. I also noted non-written communication, such as images and GIFs. Finally, I compared the themes from each platform for each event t⌐ one another. In the following sections, I note the differences and similarities between different platform communications for each event, along with overarching themes.

I am also inspired by the approach of discourse analysis. In discourse analysis, the text itself is analyzed, of course. Its form, arguments, metaphors, etc., are all considered. But then, as Nielsen and Nørreklit (2009) suggest, the researcher considers how the text fits into larger discursive patterns and practices. In other words, discourse is "a social practice which constructs social identities, social relations and the knowledge and meaning systems of the social world," according to Norman Fairclough (Nielsen, Nørreklit, 204). I also employed a similar approach analyzing the mass media texts which emerged after the 2018 midterm elections. Using the ProQuest NewsBank and Major Dallies database systems, I collected 104 texts for analysis. News texts included major national newspapers, national online sources, and cable news transcripts which mentioned Latinx voters. Parameters used to narrow down the original search results included a time frame (two weeks after the midterm election), excluding local papers, and excluding Spanish language sources. Analysis was done qualitatively and thematically, using some basic descriptive statistics.

Outline of chapters

This book addresses the overarching question of *how do U.S. Latinx advocacy organizations shape Latinx identity in the digital era of communication and the racialized public sphere of the 2010s while pursuing their goal of voter mobilization?* The past few paragraphs previewed the conceptual framework utilized in this book. In the next chapter, Chapter 2, I discuss the mediation of Latinx identity in the pre-Internet era in more depth. I discuss the theoretical genealogy of the processes of mediated Latinx identity in the mass media era.

In Chapter 3, I discuss how digital technologies have impacted the process of Latinx identity mediation from a theoretical perspective. I look at how the frames of identity formation change or adapt with digital tools and practices. In Chapter 4, I discuss how alongside Latinx cultural change, U.S. politics has also changed dramatically in between 2000 and 2018. The adoption and innovation of digital technologies by political campaigns and parties have brought up a whole host of issues.

The first research question, which will be addressed extensively in Chapter 5, is as follows: *How do organizations strategically construct a vision of U.S. Latinx identity?* Part of organizing communities into political markets involves developing a consumer identity. In general, the erasure of difference and the elevation of an essentialistic identity are important to create an audience that knows when they are being addressed. For Latinxs, this involves creating a discourse that reinterprets history and shapes identity. In Chapter 5, I also consider the role individual stakeholders play in Latinx organization regarding identity making. Here, I am curious about how actors within organizations generate knowledge and formulate heuristics about their audience. I'm also reflective on how their communication decisions are shaped by organizational mission, group culture, personal backgrounds, and a common feature of advocacy organizations: the use of national conferences to create networks and set agendas.

Chapter 6 focuses on the question of: *How are digital platforms used as sites of mobilizing Latinx voters, and how is identity reified and/or challenged on them?* While Chapter 5 is centered on the analysis of human subjects, Chapter 6 is focused on the analysis of digital products. Among the organizations studied in this work, there was a growing sentiment in the time after the 2016 election that digital tools were not the complete answer to mobilizing voters. They all recognized the power of online organizing to reach new audiences and share messages but were thinking about new arrangements of local grassroots groups and national organizations. This type of thinking about online tools and digital platforms is in line with recent research from Karpf (2016) and others. In this question, I am both interested in how the platforms are being used and how discourses of identity are shaped on the platforms. I also consider the question of platform choice and expertise. In this section, I use information and themes gained from interviews with stakeholders to analyze media messages from online platforms, such as emails and social media posts. I also ask, how are digital tools used to listen to audiences. Organizations use online media to listen to their audiences and stay connected to developments in the public sphere. The DACA and immigration policy turmoil of early 2018 exemplified the mixing of online listening habits and traditional organizing.

In Chapter 7, I look at the results of the 2018 midterms and analyze the exit polling of Latinx voters along with the rhetoric surrounding Latinx voters in the news media. I *ask how did media coverage of the 2018 midterm election reinforce the themes introduced in previous chapters?* Media largely reinforce the themes of U.S. Latinx racialization outlined in other chapters.

Finally, in Chapter 8, I restate the main findings of my work and discuss the results on theory and the field. I also conclude the study with policy suggestions and possible directions for further research around the discourses of Latinx identity in the United States. The much-heralded arrival of Latinx people onto the stage isn't a political accident; it has important implications for the racial order of the United States and for our conceptions of a diverse deliberative democracy. The rhetorical newness of the category is key. Political actors who seek to mobilize Latinx voting engage in strategic essentialism—the effort to increase a racialized political cohesion around certain issues (immigration, healthcare, etc.) toward specific political outcomes.

Notes

1 DACA refers to an executive order from the Obama administration named Deferred Action for Childhood Arrivals. In practice, it is an administrative program that places a qualifying population of immigrants at the bottom of the priority list for deportation. Recipients also receive some limited paperwork that allows them to legally work in the country. To qualify, immigrants must have arrived in the United States before a certain age and either be employed or in school. This population of immigrant recipients is sometimes called the Dreamers; however, the terms are not always used synonymously. The Obama administration promulgated DACA after several other immigration reforms had failed in Congress. The Trump administration signaled their intent to end DACA in late 2017 and asked Congress to provide a legislative fix. As of late 2018, there was no fix.

2 TPS refers to Temporary Protected Status. TPS was established as part of the Immigration Act of 1990 for humanitarian purposes. The Secretary of Homeland Security can decide to extend TPS to people in countries experiencing severe conflict and social turmoil. Recipients often are fleeing violence. The largest group of TPS recipients are refugees from El Salvador. The situation in El Salvador is bad, partly a result of natural disasters, gang warfare, and U.S. policy toward Central America. In 2018, the Trump administration announced that it would end TPS for Salvadorans in the United States.

References

Abramowitz, A. I. (2010). Transformation and polarization: The 2008 presidential election and the new American electorate. *Electoral Studies, 29*(4), 594–603. doi:10.1016/j.electstud.2010.04.006

Barreto, M. A., & Segura, G. M. (2014). *Latino America: How America's most dynamic population is poised to transform the politics of the nation.* New York, NY: PublicAffairs.

Beltran, C. (2010). *The trouble with unity: Latino politics and the creation of identity.* Oxford, UK: Oxford University Press.

Bernard, H., & Ryan, G. (1998). Text analysis: Qualitative and quantitative methods. In H. Bernard (Ed.), *Handbook of methods in cultural anthropology* (pp. 595–645). Walnut Creek, CA: AltaMira Press.

Bruns, A., & Burgess, J. (2012). Researching news discussion on Twitter. *Journalism Studies, 13*(5–6), 801–814. doi:10.1080/1461670x.2012.664428

Chadwick, A. (2013). *The hybrid media system: Politics and power.* Oxford, UK: Oxford University Press.

Chavez, C. A. (2013). Building a "new Latino" in the post-network era: Mun2 and the reconfiguration of the U.S. Latino audience. *International Journal of Communication, 7,* 1026–1045.

Chavez, L. R. (2013). *The Latino threat: Constructing immigrants, citizens, and the nation.* Stanford, CA: Stanford University Press.

Dávila, A. M. (2012). *Latinos, Inc: The marketing and making of a people.* Berkeley, CA: University of California Press.

Freebody, P. (2002). *Qualitative research in education: An introduction.* London, UK: SAGE.

Frey, L. R., Botan, C. H., & Kreps, G. L. (2007). *Investigating communication: An introduction to research methods.* Boston, MA: Allyn & Bacon.

Karpf, D. (2012). *The MoveOn effect: The unexpected transformation of American political advocacy.* Oxford, UK: Oxford University Press.

Karpf, D. (2016). *Analytic activism: Digital listening and the new political strategy.* Oxford, UK: Oxford University Press.

Kawulich, B. B. (2005). Participant Observation as a Data Collection Method. *Forum Qualitative Sozialforschung/Forum: Qualitative Social Research, 6*(2), Art. 43.

Lofland, J., Snow, D. A., Anderson, L., & Lofland, L. H. (2009). *Analyzing social settings: A guide to qualitative observation and analysis.* Belmont, CA: Wadsworth.

Marshall, C., & Rossman, G. B. (2016). *Designing qualitative research.* Los Angeles, CA: SAGE.

Mora, G. C. (2014). *Making Hispanics: How activists, bureaucrats, and media constructed a new American.* Chicago, IL: University of Chicago Press.

Nielsen, A. E., & Nørreklit, H. (2009). A discourse analysis of the disciplinary power of management coaching. *Society and Business Review, 4*(3), 202–214. doi:10.1108/17465680910994209

Patten, E. (2016, April 10). The nation's Latino population is defined by its youth. Retrieved October 31, 2018, from http://www.pewhispanic.org/2016/04/20/the-nations-latino-population-is-defined-by-its-youth/

Rodriguez, A. (1999). *Making Latino news: Race, language, class.* Thousand Oaks, CA: Sage.

Soto-Vásquez, A. D. (2018). The rhetorical construction of U.S. Latinos by American presidents. *Howard Journal of Communications*, 1–15. doi:10.1080/10646175.2017.1407718

Taylor, P., Gonzalez-Barrera, A., Passel, J., & Lopez, M. (2012, November 14). An awakened giant: The Hispanic electorate is likely to double by 2030. Retrieved October 31, 2018, from http://www.pewhispanic.org/2012/11/14/an-awakened-giant-the-hispanic-electorate-is-likely-to-double-by-2030/

Vallejo, J. A. (2012). *Barrios to burbs: The making of the Mexican American middle class.* Stanford, CA: Stanford University Press.

2 The mediation of Latinx identity before the Internet

Scholars have long sought to identify the relationship between mass media portrayals and Latinx identity. In this chapter, I outline the three themes of U.S. Latinx identity formation—the minimization of difference, denationalization, and racialization. I contextualize these three themes of U.S. Latinx identity formation with a special focus on the deployment of mass communication technologies as mechanisms of racial identity construction. As a scholar of communication theory, I theorize Latinx identity formation as an extension of framing. Framing is a theory common to many social science fields, but especially useful in communication. Entman (1993) defines framing as the selection of certain aspects of a perceived reality and making it salient. In other words, framing is the process of making some parts of a phenomenon more visible than other parts. The effect of framing will define a problem to be solved, infer a relationship, and often suggest a solution to the problem.

The news media frames events every time they report the news. Multiple frames can even be applied to the same news event. For example, let us imagine hypothetically a man shoots several people at a restaurant. One news outlet may choose to frame the story as another incident of mass shootings in the United States. Another may focus on the identity of the shooter to construct a frame of racial violence. Both frames suggest certain political courses of action too. The first suggests gun control. The second, being tough on crime.

In other words, "the frame determines whether most people notice and how they understand and remember a problem, as well as how they evaluate and choose to act upon it" (Entman, 54). Following up on Entman's discussion of framing, Scheufele (1999) adds some nuance to how framing can be used in communication research. He argues that frames can be applied to both the media and the individual. In other words, the media may apply frames as Entman argues, but individuals may also apply their own frames onto media as they consume it. In addition, frames can be researched both as independent and dependent variables. These four dimensions create a typology of potential research questions. For example, researching media frames as a dependent variable would provoke a question around which factors may influence the particular framing of an issue. The idea that in framing certain characteristics are selected to be particularly salient is especially useful for understanding why certain features of Latinx identity are highlighted and then interpreted as foundational.

The literature on the formation of U.S. Latinx identity primarily describes a process that originates from actors working within a mass media ecosystem. We obviously operate in a very different system now, where the mass media and digital media coexist. There has not yet been an attempt to explain how Latinx identity forms in a system like ours today. In this chapter, I draw from the theories of Rodriguez, Dávila, Mora, Beltrán (2010), and others to develop my own theoretical framework that describes how Latinx identity formation happened in a pre-Internet era to then think about how it changes in a multimedia, hybrid, and online media ecosystem.

A note on terminology

I have used the term *Latinx* in this book to refer to a demographic category of people in the United States. The general public will typically use the terms *Hispanic* and *Latino* interchangeably and usually without much thought about the different historical legacies of each term. Before the substance of this chapter, there is some background context to cover for the terms *Hispanic* and *Latino*. First, while the terms are used interchangeably, they have their own unique histories. Both terms are used by communities to identify themselves. They are also terms used by those with power to categorize people for political purposes. The Pew Research Center has found that the use of the terms *Hispanic* and *Latino* varies by generation and that about 10%–25% identify themselves using the pan-ethnic term *Latino*. The vast majority of Latinxs use their national identity (Mexican, American, etc.) to identify themselves. I, in this book, default to using the non-gendered (Salinas, Lozano, 2017) term *Latinx* except in cases where I am referring to a specific text (such as a book title) or group of people. I do this to be as inclusive as possible in my labeling.

Second, these are all constructed categories—*social imaginaries* that racialize people in the United States as different from others based on a sense of shared culture and other significant markers of difference.

This chapter explores the process of socializing communities of people with ancestry from Latin America in the United States into a distinct racial group. Famed Chicano historian Rodolfo Acuña has argued that people of Latin American descent are too heterogenous to be categorized using an overarching category such as Latino (2004). Thus, in this section, I will primarily use the term *Latinx* as shorthand to refer to the general grouping of people who have ancestry from Latin America and are included in the racial project I am analyzing. My use of this term is separate from the process I am discussing in detail, which I will refer to as U.S. Latinx identity formation.

Third, the development of U.S. Latinx identity is intimately tied both to transnational flows of migration from Latin America into the United States and to the quickened asymmetrical flow of capital and information across national borders. Before 1990, the Latinx population in the United States was relatively small. Shifts occurring after 1990 toward manufacturing in the global south and free trade agreements with Latin America (through trade deals like the North American Free Trade Agreement), along with an accelerating drug war, caused an increase in immigration to the United States (De la Garza, DeSipio, 2015). This dramatically increased the profile of Latinxs in the political landscape. Population growth of Latinxs is now driven by births in the United States; however, the rhetoric of Latinxs being foreign and separate to the nation remains.

Thus, in this chapter, I focus mostly on developments within the United States and within a specific time frame: the latter half of the 20th century and into the 21st century. Some may accurately argue that this time period doesn't consider the longer history of Latin America and the United States. Since the recent growth of the Latinx population is a new phenomenon, I chose to focus on this time specific with more detail. Focusing specifically on this era (roughly 1960–Present) also allows me to consider how the communication technologies of mass media facilitate the process of U.S. Latinx identity formation in a variety of different ways. The relevance of this time period and the technological changes present in it are explained in more detail in the next section.

Contextualizing the political and economic moment

This chapter explains the historical construction of Latinx identity in the United States from the mid-20th century to the early 21st century. Placed in a historical context, this period also corresponds with the political and economic transition in the United States and other parts of the world from a Fordist model of capital accumulation to a post-Fordist system. Fordism is a system of economic production in a capitalist society where standardized goods can be produced at a low cost. The Fordist system also provides enough wages for its workers to purchase the goods. In the United States, this system of production lasted until the 1970s, when a series of global economic shocks, along with political reactions against the welfare state, shifted capitalistic production.

The 1970s and 1980s held the beginnings of what is generally referred to as neo-liberal economics and politics. Manufacturing, or Fordist production, shifted to the global south. This shift, in combination with the degradation of the welfare state, led to the gradual transfer of wealth from the working and middle classes to the wealthy. The industries that remained in the United States were generally split into two sectors. The first was a low-wage service sector where workers were often part-time, at-will employees with no benefits. The second sector was a creative and professional sector where entry was tightly controlled by educational credentials and social capital. These sectors of the economy were emboldened by the deregulation and anti-unionization of most industries at the end of the 20th century. This flexible model of accumulation is sometimes called late capitalism, which also includes the primacy of the market in everyday life (Harvey, 1991).

The production of identity as a commodity like oil or steel is critical to the transformation of society in the postmodern era. Identity becomes a commodity to be consumed and produced, except that it is often immaterial in form. Identity as a commodity places the development of U.S. Latinx identity within the context of a globalized postmodern political economy. The innovation of communication technologies, which compresses the distance between people and lessen the time it takes to convey information, also plays a critical role in the development of Latinx identity across many different groups of people.

Racial formation theory applied

Latinx identity in the United States can best be understood as an ongoing racial commodity project, rather than a fixed essential category of people. Racial formation theorists understand race as a political project. Racialization is the process of making race real. Looking specifically at the black/white racial binary formation of the United States, Omi and Winant (2015) define race as a signifying concept that represents the social conflict and interests relating to differing types of human bodies. The selection of physical features that signify racial difference are always political choices, since race has no biological basis (172). In the United States, black/white racial binary, skin color, hair texture, and other phenotypes serve as powerful markers of difference. The selection of Latinx physical phenotypes is less clear and thus produces both confusion and reliance on cultural markers of difference, such as language, food, and dress.

Racialization began as an Enlightenment-era project to justify colonization, resource extraction from the new world to the old world, and the labor exploitation of colonized people. In effect, the concept of race became a tool of colonizers to control populations. In the early history of the United States, it was necessary to divide the colonized and enslaved subjects by race to conform with the on-paper notion that all men were created equally. Racial inferiority was used to justify the unequal and inhumane treatment of indigenous and enslaved peoples by economic elites. Indentured whites were an early ally of enslaved Africans in early U.S. history. Events like Bacon's Rebellion, where poor whites and enslaved blacks joined together to rebel against the economic elites of the time, are a clear example. Cooper (2001) has argued that Bacon's Rebellion was a major impetus for the deployment of racial ideology by the ruling class to divide and conquer the poor and prevent further class-based uprisings.

For most of its history after the United States largely existed in a black/white binary of understanding race. The recent rhetorical arrival of Latinxs in the nation challenges this black/white binary as well as the racial system of the United States since the black/white binary was developed in a less sophisticated mass-media era. Omi and Winant see "the meaning of race [as] open to many types of agency, from the individual to the organizational, from the local to the global" (181). In an era of unprecedented ability to communicate online, the ongoing racial formation of the "emerging" Latinx community is a fertile topic to investigate. Omi and Winant understand "racial formation as the intersectional conflict of racial 'projects' that combine representational and discursive elements with structural/institutional ones" (181), which opens up wide-ranging investigative potential.

Racial formation occurs at multiple levels of society. The culture industry produces images of Latinx identity easily consumable by mainstream audiences—from early representations of Puerto Ricans in *West Side Story* (Negrón-Muntaner, 2000) to the sultry characters played by Sofía Vergara in film and TV (Vidal-Ortiz, 2016). Latinas are often presented as spicy characters with hot tempers and even hotter sex drives. The Latina body has long been represented, even since the silent film era, as sexualized and available to the appetites of U.S. men (Mendible, 2007). Latinas often represent a contradictory balance between foreign and familiar, exotic but common. This is reinforced through the presentation of characters like Jenifer Lopez as a maid in *Maid in Manhattan* and America Ferrera as an everyday *chica* next door in *Ugly Betty* (Molina-Guzmán, 2010). Latinx men are not safe either; they are presented as either drug dealers or criminals. The lack of Latinx media producers ends up limiting the presentation of Latinx subjects in film and television to one-dimensional stereotypes.

Audiences, both mainstream and marginal, also reproduce stereotypical representations in their imagination of Latinx bodies. Consider the success Donald Trump enjoyed in the 2016 presidential election following a campaign in which he cast Mexican immigrants as rapists and criminals. His calls to build a wall on the United States/Mexico border were certainly reminiscent of Hollywood films such as *Sicario* and *No Country for Old Men*, which cast the borderlands as a violent, lawless space. If a Trump voter's image of what the border looks like is based on the violent shootouts between cartel members featured in both *Sicario* and *No Country for Old Men*, then the logic of building a wall and limiting immigration seems clear and necessary.

Political actors along the ideological spectrum use Latinxs to advance their agendas (Soto-Vásquez, 2018). In my work on this subject, I have looked at how U.S. presidents have used Latinx subject naming and categorization to advance their agendas. For politicians using Latinx subjects in the 2016 and 2018 elections this included depicting Latinxs as criminalized figures in nativist anti-immigrant rhetoric to mobilize the right and as passive voters in the Democratic coalition.

Large business interests market to both Spanish-dominant and bilingual Latinx audiences, while small entrepreneurs serve local Latinx markets across the country. Marketers and advertisers have long tried to figure how to cater to Latinxs' $1.5 trillion purchasing power. In "Making Latino News: Race, Language, and Class" (1999), América Rodriguez builds a useful framework to uncover the ongoing attempt to construct a pan-ethnic, denationalized, and racialized Latinx entity in the United States by news media producers and news making institutions. While Rodriguez looked at Spanish language news, both English language and Spanish language news media develop homogenized, stereotypical representations of Latinxs. For example, Correa (2010) found that English language news tended to present the achievements of Latinas as emblematic of their ethnicity achieving success in the United States and "described them as a profitable new market" (425). Spanish language news, however, framed successful Latinas as making family-oriented sacrifices to achieve their goals. Both media organizations played into stereotypes, even if they arrived at different outcomes.

In addition, other scholars have correctly pointed out that national origin identifiers, such as Cuban and Mexican, are constructed per the interests of Latin American states' imaginaries (Grosfoguel, Georas, 2000). National identity is the preeminent "imagined community," in the words of Benedict Anderson (1983). Nations are "imagined because the members of even the smallest nation will never know most of their fellow-members, meet them, or even hear of them, yet in the minds of each lives the image of their communion" (6). The crux of Anderson's argument on the rise of national identity in the late 19th century is the development of the first mass media, such as newspapers, during the industrial revolution. Again, it is clear that the development of new communication technologies is connected to the model of economic production of that era. Thankfully, many Latinx thinkers before me have charted a path toward uncovering the three dimensions of the political, media, and economic production of Latinx identity.

Minimization of difference

U.S. Latinx identity is a racial abstraction, where *difference is minimized* and similarities are highlighted for political and economic benefits. The minimization of difference is a common feature of politics and political campaign. By necessity, individuals and groups are amalgamated into constituencies. For example, think of all the diversity that exists within an imagined political constituency such as the "white working class." The highlighting of salient similarities can also be thought of as an example of framing. A similar process happens to Latinx populations in the United States, except that the minimization of difference happens at the most fundamental levels of physical characteristics, body types, and culture. Physical phenotypes across Latin American populations are tremendously diverse due to the legacy of colonization. For example, one Latinx person may be light skinned with blonde hair, while another may be dark skinned with black hair. Since physical phenotypes are less easily categorized, cultural similarities are typically used as unifying features instead.

Historically, the Spanish language served as the primary signifier of pan-ethnic abstraction in the United States. Specifically, Rodriguez states that, "from a marketing perspective, the Spanish language is what makes the Hispanic audience efficient" (18) in Spanish language news. This efficiency guarantees that advertising and audience construction utilizing the Spanish language exclusively targets Latinxs. The dominance of Spanish throughout Latin America is a result of Spanish colonization of the continent and the slow but methodical elimination and marginalization of indigenous languages. This cultural dominance is also reflected in the term *Hispanic*, used to signify pan-ethnic identity.

From the rise of Spanish marketing in the 1960s until the 21st century, the assumption was that *Latino* and *Hispanic* meant Spanish-speaking. As successive generations of Latinxs assimilated into the culture of the United States, English became more dominant. Some national Latinx organizations have historically emphasized the use of English in the official proceedings as well. Media organizations have responded in kind since the 2000s. Fusion was launched as a bilingual television network in the 2010s by ABC and Univision. Comcast launched Mun2, a bilingual take on the Spanish language network Telemundo. Univision has also experimented with introducing English-speaking characters into their Spanish language *novelas* as well as providing English subtitles in an attempt to market to younger Latinxs (Young, 2012).

Dávila notes in her work on Hispanic marketing that the structural difficulty of conveying meaning in a 30-second advertisement necessarily "brings to the surface the tropes, images, and discourses that have become widespread as generalized representations of Hispanidad" (14). Generalized representation crosses ethnic, racial, and cultural lines in mediated representation. A prominent example is Jennifer Lopez playing iconic Tejano singer Selena in the eponymous biopic. The casting of Lopez, who is Puerto Rican, as a Mexican American set off a minor controversy among fans of the singer. For Aparicio (2003), the casting of Lopez as Selena creates a space that enables critics to critique the homogenization of Latinxs and also find similarities between different Latinx populations. More recent productions have continued to cast Latinxs in roles haphazardly. Brazilian actor Wagner Moura portrayed Colombian drug lord Pablo Escobar in *Narcos* despite having to learn Spanish for the role. For Spanish speakers with an ear for regional accents, Moura's imitation of a *paisa* accent was out of place. Meanwhile, mainstream audiences may have failed to notice the accent difference amid visions of Colombia crafted by the Netflix producers.

Class identity and knowledge production plays an important role here too. Early Hispanic marketing firms, primarily founded by Cuban American exiles, used the pan-ethnic categorization to secure advertising budgets from mainstream brands (Dávila, 2012, 23–34). Using market research, which mostly projected their economically privileged social status onto all Latinxs, these early firms founded in the 1970s laid the groundwork for the current understanding of Latinxs in the United States. This meant characterizing all Latinxs as socially conservative, family-oriented, and very brand loyal. This essentializing of U.S. Latinxs was used to convince mainstream brands that Latinxs were worth advertising to as a unique market. The uniqueness of the Latinx market was reinforced by the knowledge production that the marketing firms used to justify their work (56–63). This included the full range of knowledge production technologies, such as focus groups, surveys, and other research methods. Limited data and logical leaps in findings then came to reinforce the preconceived notions of Latinx identity.

De Genova and Ramos-Zayas (2008) summarize these processes in their article "Latino Racial Formations": "Both the Latino and Hispanic labels, but especially the more aggressively de-politicized Hispanic label, increasingly became hegemonic categories of capital with the construction and cultivation of specialized Spanish-speaking market segments" (5). The construction and cultivation of the Spanish-speaking market in the United States stood vis-à-vis the Latinx market. The advertising and marketing communications technologies Dávila refers to go beyond the mere construction of stereotypical images of Latinxs. Instead, her work demonstrates the process of commodified culture production typical of the late-capitalist system. Traditional cultural practices, such as the traditional worship of religious icons and musical expression, become means to create affective responses in Latinx audiences to motivate consumption in late-capitalist production.

The erasure of difference in Latinx racialization also elevates the cultural features of the majority group in the category: Mexican Americans. As mentioned earlier, at one level, there is a minimization of political difference. Immigration is classified as a "Latinx issue," even though it does not affect all populations equally. At a micro level, patterns of immigration to the United States are challenging cultural conceptions of Latinidad. Mayan immigrants from rural Guatemala to rural Georgia struggle to maintain their cultural heritage not only against homogenizing U.S. mainstream culture but also against homogenizing Mexican culture (Lebaron, 2012). Elders in the Mayan immigrant community worry that their children are adopting Mexican and Latinx cultural attitudes to gain social status, even if it is slightly less marginal status. Lebaron notes that Mayan youth in Georgia signal their identity by consuming Mexican cultural products (like *Norteño* music). Thus, the minimization of difference occurs both at the level of production of culture and at the level of consumption of culture.

In summary, difference is highly present among populations of people normally grouped into the Latinx category. This difference is minimized, and sometimes completely erased, for the purposes of maintaining a cohesive Latinx identity in the United States. These differences are often minimized for marketing and efficiency purposes in commercial media. In addition, certain differences are more likely to be minimized. Racial and ethnic difference, especially in the case of African and Indigenous heritage, is downplayed. Latinxs in the media or in political office end up looking like an unrepresentative portion of Latinxs. They tend to have physical features typically associated with European Americans. They also tend to be from the professional class—well educated and with more economic resources. This disjunction between the leadership of the Latinx community and the people they claim to represent emerges as a theme in Chapters 4 and 5.

Denationalization

Denationalization refers to a process in which national identity (Mexican, Colombian, Dominican, etc.) is shed to assimilate and create "U.S. Latinxs." Rodriguez comments that "the production of Latino journalism—news that is purposefully and strategically created for U.S. residents of Latin American descent symbolically denationalizes Latinos, as it renationalizes them as U.S. Hispanics" (15). Here, Rodriguez also points out that the production of news by a certain class of Latinxs colors the creation of Latinx political issues. Journalists tend to be more highly educated and hold higher economic status than their audiences. I made a similar point in the previous section, on the minimization of difference, noting how Latinxs in the mass media look quite different from their audiences. However, there is a distinction between denationalization and the minimization of difference, since the nationality of Latinxs plays a major role in their lived realities. The denationalization and renationalization of Latinxs are, as seen in the example from Rodriguez, done through a process of agenda setting. Issues relating to the United States are presented in the news and media, domesticating Latinxs into their new homeland. These issues, such as immigration and minority status, are then framed as Latinx issues.

As mentioned earlier, immigration as a political issue is strongly framed in media as a Latinx issue. For example, during the Jorge Ramos–Donald Trump controversy, when Trump ejected Ramos from a press conference after Ramos repeatedly asked for details on his proposed deportation plan, the terms *Latinx* and *Mexican* were used interchangeably. Ramos was simultaneously described as the most trusted anchor by Mexican Americans and by Latinxs—as if the two populations could be overlaid completely. The assumption in the press became that Trump, through his rhetoric targeting Mexican immigrants, had offended *all Latinxs* and would subsequently receive an electoral backlash. The results from 2016 exit polls are inconclusive, but they matter less than the rhetorical tying of Mexican American and Mexican immigrant issues to Latinx issues.

In *The Trouble with Unity*, Cristina Beltrán provides a theoretical account of the Chicano and Puerto Rican movements in the 1960s and 1970s and the eventual transformation of those national identity–based movements into a "project of unity" (1–5). The project of unity, which Beltran critiques, aims to politically unite different groups of Latinxs into a voting bloc that can organize for resources and representation. Here, the denationalization of Latinxs was tied to the specific aim of depoliticizing the Chicano and Puerto Rican civil rights movements of 1960s. The National Council of La Raza (NCLR), founded originally as a Mexican American organization, expanded to represent all Latinxs in 1975. The civil rights era of the Chicano and Puerto Rican movements also saw specific efforts to mobilize voters. The Southwest Voter Registration Education Project (SVREP), founded in 1974 in San Antonio, deployed grassroots tactics to organize Mexican American voters in South Texas. They have also since expanded their work to include all Latinxs.

This call to represent all Latinxs happened concurrently with the rise of the pan-ethnic term *Hispanic* in official and popular rhetoric. NCLR solidified as a national organization by including Puerto Rican and Cuban American organizations. NCLR and other organizations then negotiated alongside other groups, including Univision, with the federal government to create the census category Hispanic (Mora, 2014). The beginnings of a project of Latinx unity in official U.S. politics followed in the decades after. Organizations like NCLR began striving for professionalism and became less activist and more lobbyist in their approach (Ortiz, 1997). In 2017, NCLR announced rebranded themselves as UnidosUS. This rebrand further distanced them from their initial founding as an organization for Mexican Americans.

In *Hispanics in Congress* (1996), Maurilio Vigil explains that the Congressional Hispanic Caucus (CHC) was founded as a legislative service in the U.S. House of Representatives and eventually became an organization for Latinx representatives to advance "a Hispanic agenda." Vigil notes that the original hope of the CHC was that Hispanic identity could bring together members from both parties along with different geographic regions representing different people. This proved to be a failure. Republican members of the group eventually refused to go along with the policy agenda of the larger CHC (dominated by Democrats) and left to form their own organization.

Latinxs are not only denationalized from their sending countries; as Rodriguez points out, they are also renationalized as U.S. Americans. Nationalization as U.S. Americans envisions Latinxs as "supportive of U.S. society's structures and norms, and yet also apart from it, preserving a distinct Latino identity" (17). Their nationalization makes them a minority group within U.S. society, and therefore they are constituted "as marginal members" (22). As such, the politics of Latinxs takes the form of a clear power differential in which they must petition those with resources for help. And how do people actually use the term *Latino*? The Pew Hispanic Center indicates that 51% of U.S. Latinxs identify with their national origin rather than an overarching pan-ethnic identity. Moreover, 69% cannot define an overarching "Hispanic culture," and 51% don't see themselves as fitting into standard racial categories. Finally, and perhaps ironically, only 14% prefer the term *Latino* as an identifier (Taylor, Lopez, Martínez, Velasco, 2012).

Latinx political action in the United States can be categorized in three distinct eras.[1] First, the *era of legitimacy* extends from 19th-century U.S. imperialism to the end of World War II. During this phase, Latinxs in the United States struggled to demonstrate their citizenship to the state in a white-dominated society. While the Treaty of Guadalupe Hidalgo granted nominal citizenship status to Mexicans living in the newly acquired territory of the Southwest, their citizenship was second class at best. Voting and employment discrimination were widespread throughout the Southwest. In South Texas, land was confiscated, and many Mexicans lived under the threat of violence. The colonization of Puerto Rico imposed a different type of second-class citizenship on its people. One of the earliest Latinx civic organizations, the League of United Latin American Citizens (LULAC), founded in 1929, explicitly emphasized in its rhetoric the "Americanness" of Latinxs (Dowling, 2014). The struggle to demonstrate citizenship culminated in World War II, with millions of young Latinx men fighting for the U.S. armed services overseas. Those who returned from war confronted racism and prejudice back home and organized into groups such as the American G.I. Forum. They emphasized Latinx veterans' service to the nation as a call for political and economic rights to housing, voting, and jobs.

The era of legitimacy for Latinx groups in the United States followed a specific logic: to attain the civil and political rights guaranteed to all citizens by the Constitution, Latinxs should closely align themselves with the ideology and symbols of the nation. This even included a push to classify Latinxs as racially white to secure civil rights in a segregated society. To this day, LULAC and the G.I. Forum heavily emphasize the U.S. flag, the national anthem, and military service. They use service and fidelity to the country to argue for their inclusion in it.

The social change and upheaval of the 1960s heralded the *era of protest*. As mentioned earlier, social movements made specific political demands upon U.S. structures of power. Organizations founded in this era include NCLR and others. The era of protest included strikes, marches, and countless hours of hard work in the *lucha*. Cesar Chavez and Dolores Huerta famously led the farmworker's rights protests in California. In the Southwest, the Chicano movement flourished in the 1960s. An important idea developed during this time period was that of *Aztlán*, which was understood as the mythical, ancestral homeland of Chicanos. The development of *Aztlán* was an important step in developing Chicano nationalism, a sense of identity apart from being Mexican or U.S. American. This sense of being *ni de aqui, ni de alla*, meaning neither from here (the United States) nor from there (Latin America), became an important part of Latinx identity in the following years.

The era of protest was not limited to Mexican Americans either. The 1960s also saw social movements of Puerto Ricans in urban environments like Chicago and New York City. A group of young *puertorriqueños* called the Young Lords mobilized their communities around housing and other forms of discrimination (Wanzer-Serrano, 2015). In 1970, the Young Lords outlined their major goals, which included a commitment to self-determination of *puertorriqueños* and all Latinxs. They also advocated for a commitment to anti-racism and anti-misogyny and an embrace of socialist politics. The latter half of the era of protest saw the mobilization of Latinxs around their representation in the media. Montgomery (1990) notes how Latinx advocacy groups like NCLR and LULAC pressured Frito-Lay to end the character the "Frito Bandito," who was viewed as a racist caricature, and were successful. Other Latinx groups, in coordination with other advocates, pressured mass media producers to change the way they portrayed Latinx subjects.

In a drastic departure following the confrontation of the 1960s and early 1970s, the *era of assimilation* dominated Latinx political action until the 2010s. In this era, the overarching pan-ethnic label of *Hispanic* was introduced. Political action was undertaken to integrate

Latinxs into the political and economic fabric of the United States. From advertising and marketing to the project of unity, as Dávila and Beltrán note, respectively, Latinxs became one body—separate from the mainstream but closer than before. There are a couple of reasons for this shift. Many of the leaders of the Chicano, Puerto Rican, and other advocacy groups either died or burned out. The federal government also cracked down on activist groups, associating them with radical political activity to disrupt their work.

In part, the successes of the era of protest also enabled its end. The landmark federal court case *Mendez v. Westminster* enabled Mexican Americans to attend desegregated schools. Other achievements of the civil rights era opened up new opportunities for Latinxs. As Latinxs entered higher education and the professional workforce, they encountered discrimination. Often, the response to discrimination was to assimilate to mainstream values and culture to get along.

The current era is less clear. Two possibilities are apparent for Latinx political action in an era of renewed and reenergized nativism, racism, and xenophobia. The first possibility is a *renewed era of protest* and activism to combat eroding civil rights and rising white nationalism using the communication technologies of the era to unite disparate groups and build coalitions of people. The second possibility is an *era of fragmentation*, also partly a result of new communication technologies, where disparate interest groups of Latinxs advance their own agendas. These potential eras also closely mirror the affordances associated with the Internet and online organizing that I raised in Chapter 1. Fragmentation may also explain the challenges of mobilizing a mass Latinx constituency.

Racialization

Finally, the *racialization* of U.S. Latinxs refers to the disregard of racial difference highly present in Latin America and the process of constituting Latinxs in the United States as a racial group along the lines of white and black. Here, Rodriguez comments, "Similarly, race (and racial categorizing) is also the product of social processes. The conceptualization of U.S. people of Latin American descent as a race (think of the phrase 'Blacks and Hispanics') erases the multiracial and multicultural heritage of these communities—both north and south of the Rio Grande" (18). Latinxs' racial identity plays an important role in their political action. When Latinxs are racialized as a group separate from whites and blacks, there is a confrontation with the black/white racial binary of the United States.

Sometimes, Latinxs are colloquially included in a coalition of people of color (POC). This overarching identity is formed in opposition to whites as an othering process. Recently, this process has come under scrutiny as activists have noted that some Latinxs also benefit from white privilege while identifying as POC. In essence, they are racial double-dippers—able to benefit from positive identification as Latinx while retreating into white privilege otherwise. The ambiguity of the terms *Hispanic, Latina/o*, and *Latinx* also plays a role in racial double-dipping. The racialization of Latinxs as a separate minority group with the simultaneous disregard for difference in Latinx bodies allows for flexible articulations of identity. Latinxs with lighter skin or other physical phenotypes that signal whiteness can access certain privileges in white-dominated spaces that darker-skinned Latinxs may not be able to. Others may decide that it is in their best interest to identify culturally as a Latinx person but not associate a political ideology with their cultural identity (i.e., their identity is apolitical).

Mora (2014) chronicles the creation of the demographic category of Hispanic in the 1970s and 1980s. While in the official U.S. Census Bureau sense the term *Hispanic* functions as an ethnicity rather than a race, it is used interchangeably in practice. She argues that pan-ethnic politics "did not have to happen," since in the 1960s agenda setting between Chicano and Puerto Rican groups would typically devolve into shouting matches and hard feelings. So, what happened? Her theorization is that two factors shaped the acceptance of a new Hispanic identity. First, networks of state and non-state actors from different national backgrounds developed. These networks included "federal bureaucrats in the executive office, Census Bureau officials, activists, and media executives" (4–5). Second, she argues that the categorical ambiguity of the term eased its acceptance. There was no commonly accepted definition of the term *Hispanic*, just common cultural markers. She notes that "ambiguity was important because it allowed for stakeholders to bend the definition of Hispanic pan-ethnicity and use the notion instrumentally—as a means to an end" (5). In this way, Hispanic identity came to be reinforced though marketing budgets, as Rodriguez and Dávila show, but also though allocation of resources by the federal government. Hispanics came to be seen, because of the ambiguous definition, as separate from whites and blacks with their own demographic strata in education, income, and health issues.

The development of Hispanic, Latina/o, Latinx, etc. identity can be used to advance the agendas of their interpreters. Latinx Republicans argue that the alleged socially conservative values (think back to the market research in Dávila's work) of Latinxs, such as familial loyalty and religiosity, make them natural socially conservative Republicans. The construction of Latinxs as hardworking and entrepreneurial neatly fits into the agenda of organizations like the U.S. Hispanic Chamber of Commerce. The flexible identity interpretations of Latinxs allow for power to flow into and through Latinx populations at multiple levels.

Given these three thematic areas of theory around the production of Latinx racial identity, it is important to note that the national categories we consider as markers of difference are also constructions themselves. Mexican, Puerto Rican, Cuban, and other Latin American national identities are constructed from national racial projects, colonialism, and geo-politics. As such, De Genova and Ramos-Zayas argue that "culturalist explanations of intra-Latinx 'ethnic' identifications tend to presuppose substantive, if not essentialized, commonalities internal to groups with origins in Latin America, and thereby also take for granted their a priori status as groups" (3). So, while the political socialization of Chicano and Puerto Rican groups in the 1960s eventually led to the emergence of the pan-ethnic racial identifiers *Hispanic* and *Latino*, new immigrant groups from Latin America and new generations of those born here come into an already established racial system of white/black/Latinx in the United States.

In summary, Latinxs are also racialized as a separate group in opposition to white and black people in the United States. This totally disregards the racial difference highly present in Latin America. Racial difference is the result of colonization in the Americas and a continued social policy of racial mixing. Latinxs are othered, or marked as different, by racial discourse in the United States, and this is reinforced through government policy and media representation. The racialization does contain ambiguity. It allows for white-passing Latinxs to claim identity as POC while simultaneously benefiting from white privilege. The racialization of Latinxs as separate from black people also erases the communities of Afro-Latinxs in the United States.[2]

This chapter has outlined a historical development of U.S. Latinx identity developed through pre-Internet communication technologies. The construction of identity occurred in three primary thematic areas: the minimization of difference, denationalization, and racialization. Many of these socialization processes are intertwined and influence each other. Regardless, the end goal is the same—creating the "new Latino." That is—an identity well suited to fit into mainstream multiculturalism as a consumer. These communication processes closely follow concepts of framing and agenda setting. Certain characteristics are selected as salient and, thus, used to frame the problem (or in this case, identity problem). Later in the book, I turn to analyzing how the mobilization of the Latinx polity through digital technologies by national Latinx organizations can be understood by this conceptual framework. In the next chapter, I will focus on some of the most recent literature that discusses how Latinx identity is changed by the digital era.

Notes

1 For an unparalleled history of Chicanos in the United States, refer to *Occupied America: A history of Chicanos* by Rodolfo Acuña (2019).
2 Movements to recognize Afro-Latinxs have recently emerged. For more information, see "Afro-Latinx: A Deeply Rooted Identity among U.S. Hispanics" by López and Gonzalez-Barrera (2016).

References

Acuña, R. (2004). *U.S. Latino issues.* Westport, CT: Greenwood Press.

Acuña, R. (2019). *Occupied America: A history of Chicanos.* Hoboken, NJ: Pearson Education.

Anderson, B. (1983). *Imagined communities: Reflections on the origin and spread of nationalism.* New York, NY: Verso.

Aparicio, F. R. (2003). Jennifer as Selena: Rethinking Latinidad in media and popular culture. *Latino Studies, 1*(1), 90–105. doi:10.1057/palgrave. lst.8600016

Beltran, C. (2010). *The trouble with unity: Latino politics and the creation of identity.* Oxford, UK: Oxford University Press.

Cooper, W. J. (2001). *Liberty and slavery: Southern politics to 1860.* Columbia, SC: University of South Carolina Press.

Correa, T. (2010). Framing Latinas: Hispanic women through the lenses of Spanish-language and English-language news media. *Journalism: Theory, Practice & Criticism, 11*(4), 425–443. doi:10.1177/1464884910367597

Dávila, A. M. (2012). *Latinos, Inc: The marketing and making of a people.* Berkeley, CA: University of California Press.

De la Garza, R. O., & DeSipio, L. (2015). *US immigration in the twenty-first century: Making Americans, remaking America.* New York, NY: Routledge.

Dowling, J. A. (2014). *Mexican Americans and the question of race.* Austin, TX: University of Texas Press.

Entman, R. M. (1993). Framing: Toward clarification of a fractured paradigm. *Journal of Communication, 43*(4), 51–58. doi:10.1111/j.1460-2466.1993. tb01304.x

Genova, N. D., & Ramos-Zayas, A. Y. (2008). Latino racial formations in the United States: An introduction. *Journal of Latin American Anthropology, 8*(2), 2–16. doi:10.1525/jlca.2003.8.2.2

Grosfoguel, R., & Georas, C. S. (2000). "Coloniality of power" and racial dynamics: Notes toward a reinterpretation of Latino Caribbeans in New York City1. *Identities, 7*(1), 85–125. doi:10.1080/1070289x.2000.9962660

Harvey, D. (1991). *The condition of postmodernity: An enquiry into the origins of cultural change.* Cambridge, MA: Wiley-Blackwell.

Lebaron, A. (2012). When Latinos are not Latinos: The case of Guatemalan Maya in the United States, the southeast and Georgia. *Latino Studies, 10*(1–2), 179–195. doi:10.1057/lst.2012.8

López, G., & Gonzalez-Barrera, A. (2016, March 01). Afro-Latino: A deeply rooted identity among U.S. Hispanics. Retrieved October 31, 2018, from http://www.pewresearch.org/fact-tank/2016/03/01/afro-latino-a-deeply-rooted-identity-among-u-s-hispanics/

Mendible, M. (2007). *From bananas to buttocks: The Latina body in popular film and culture.* Austin, TX: University of Texas Press.

Molina-Guzmán, I. (2010). *Dangerous curves: Latina bodies in the media.* New York, NY: New York University Press.

Montgomery, K. C. (1990). *Target: Prime time: Advocacy groups and the struggle over entertainment television.* Oxford, UK: Oxford University Press.

Mora, G. C. (2014). *Making Hispanics: How activists, bureaucrats, and media constructed a New American.* Chicago, IL: University of Chicago Press.

Negrón-Muntaner, F. (2000). Feeling pretty: West side story and Puerto Rican identity discourses. *Social Text, 18*(2), 83–106. doi:10.1215/01642472-18-2_63-83

Omi, M., & Winant, H. (2015). *Racial formation in the United States.* New York, NY: Routledge.

Ortiz, I. D. (1997). Chicana/o organizational politics in the era of retrenchment. In D. R. Maciel (Ed.), *Chicanas/Chicanos at the crossroads: Social, economic, and political change.* Tucson, AZ: University of Arizona Press.

Rodriguez, A. (1999). *Making Latino news: Race, language, class.* Thousand Oaks, CA: Sage.

Salinas, C., & Lozano, A. (2017). Mapping and recontextualizing the evolution of the term Latinx: An environmental scanning in higher education. *Journal of Latinos and Education,* 1–14. doi:10.1080/15348431.2017.1390464

Scheufele, D. (1999). Framing as a theory of media effects. *Journal of Communication, 49*(1), 103–122. doi:10.1093/joc/49.1.103

Soto-Vásquez, A. D. (2018). The rhetorical construction of U.S. Latinos by American presidents. *Howard Journal of Communications,* 1–15. doi:10.1080/10646175.2017.1407718

Taylor, P., Lopez, M., Martínez, J., & Velasco, G. (2012, April 4). When labels don't fit: Hispanics and their views of identity. Retrieved October 31, 2018, from http://www.pewhispanic.org/2012/04/04/when-labels-dont-fit-hispanics-and-their-views-of-identity/

Vidal-Ortiz, S. (2016). Sofía Vergara: On media representations of Latinidad. In J. A. Smith & B. K. Thakore (Eds.), *Race and contention in twenty-first century U.S. media* (pp. 85–99). New York, NY: Routledge.

Vigil, M. E. (1996). *Hispanics in congress: A historical and political survey.* Lanham, MD: University Press of America.

Wanzer-Serrano, D. (2015). *The New York young lords and the struggle for liberation.* Philadelphia, PA: Temple University Press.

Young, J. (2012, August 04). Televisa sets sights on U.S. market. Retrieved October 31, 2018, from https://variety.com/2012/tv/news/televisa-sets-sights-on-u-s-market-1118057436/

3 New media and U.S. Latinx identity

Technological and media convergence[1] has provided new opportunities for the expression of identity online. People from different backgrounds can find a corner of the Internet where they can affirm their identities. Ethnic, racial, sexual, and other minority groups, previously socially isolated, can build community online and organize (Shirky, 2009). Technological and media convergence opens up space online for these groups, and also for the mobilization of political constituencies. Campaigns and other political groups can use digital tools to reach voters and tap into grassroots energy. These next two chapters focus on the most recent literature in the field of communication related to the interrelated topics of identity construction online and political mobilization. What is not clear in academic literature is the bridge between these two topics—specifically the role identity construction plays in online political mobilization, especially for U.S. Latinx populations. My survey of the recent research shows the gap in the work done in this area.

A key theme I raised in Chapter 1 is the idea that computer-mediated communication, especially online social platforms, represents both a totalizing and disruptive force on Latinx identity formation. Online media can be used by actors to create large Latinx markets in politics or commerce. Online media can also be used as a disruptive force where other actors can question or challenge Latinx identity formation. I used the works of Latinx scholars used in Chapter 2 to synthesize and uncover the distinct facets of Latinx racial formation in the United States: *the minimization of difference, denationalization*, and *racialization*. Their work mostly focuses on the era of mass electronic communication. They show how the communication technologies of that time, including Spanish-language news, marketing and advertising, knowledge production in surveys and research, Census taking, and political organizing, played an important role in constructing U.S. Latinx identity. New technologies will undoubtedly produce new variations of racial identity, and the Latinx racial project will evolve as new communication technologies are adopted and utilized.

It is much less clear how online platforms, with their contradictory tendencies toward reification and fragmentation, will shape Latinx identity formation. I attempt to bridge that gap in this chapter. I am not advancing a technologically deterministic argument here. The development and use of electronic media mid-century did not directly cause new iterations of Latinx identity to form and be reinforced. Social diffusion of technology posits a more complex interaction between people and tech. Actors, especially those with power, use new technologies to advance their agendas in new ways. This was clear in Dávila's example of Cuban immigrants who decided to use their experience as marketers in Cuba to create a new market of Latinx consumers through television and magazine media (Dávila, 2012). For those interested in reifying Latinx racial identity in the United States, the tools of digital communication are powerful ones.

Technologies are not neutral artifacts. Politics and ideology are always embedded into their design and use (Winner, 1980). Technologies are also used according to the ideology of political action associated with the times. As Dávila points out, television advertisements were an effective tool in the era of assimilation to create a distinct but still U.S. Latinx audience. The news media, as Mora (2014) and Rodriguez (1999) mention, was also an effective tool in both the assimilation era and the current one.

The current era, whether it is a fragmented or newly reenergized protest era, also sees actors using social media to advance agendas. Social media is not massified like radio or television, where one person or group has the power to broadcast to many. Rather, the Internet is a network where information flows via strong and weak ties. The features of social media, especially algorithmic information segregation, sort communicative spaces where people are more likely to share political, ideological, and demographic similarities. This is precisely why it is unclear whether the current era will be one of fragmentation or renewed protest.

Technologies are used to advance agendas; they are tools, after all. Rather than fetishize the communications platforms themselves, it's important to focus on the politics embedded in them. There has recently been an increase of digital-first companies creating social media content for the U.S. Latinx millennial market (Aldama, 2013). Sharp video production and virility designed into the content are exemplified by videos like "7 songs at every Mexican party" or "12 reasons why Walter Mercado is the Beyoncé of Spanish TV." This media feels novel and fresh for a generation of Latinxs who grew up watching *telenovelas* with their grandparents. People get excited over the prospect of representation in media. Yet, representational politics are usually limited as commercial products since they only articulate gaining a position in the current hierarchical power structure. These new developments in media from the 2010s onward will reshape the articulations of homogenization, denationalization, and racialization, but it is unlikely that there will be any overwhelming change in the balance of power or in any embedded systems of racial difference. Latinxs' political agenda is limited in the United States if the population cannot imagine agendas beyond representational politics.

The project of unity has influenced the desire to mobilize the Latinx vote in the 2010s. The effort to speak to a broad Latinx political audience and unite different national factions around Latinx issues was adopted by the legacy organizations discussed earlier. Voto Latino has taken a youth-oriented, digital-focused effort to mobilize the Latinx vote, and other organizations have since followed suit. This identification as youth-focused and digital-content-oriented has allowed Voto Latino and organizations like it to attract significant corporate partnerships and foundational funding. The vision of a united Latinx polity is being remapped via networked communities connected digitally.

In the first section, I consider how new media possibilities, affordances, and strategies associated with the Internet converge with U.S. Latinx naming practices. I then follow up with the general navigating of online worlds by young Latinxs and then civic culture specifically. It might seem possible to liken the division between old and new media to the division between offline (or analog) and online (or digital) media. This division is not actually useful. The current media ecology is a hybrid system with interconnected parts of old and new media (Chadwick, 2013). Thus, in the literature I have selected to review in this chapter, it will be evident that the identity of U.S. Latinxs is formulated and contested in networks of traditional media production alongside audience feedback and new media content. Most of the works I review are focused on non-political activities, again reiterating our collective gap in knowledge.

A key theme that emerges through the literature in this chapter is the transformation of identity as traditionally understood into identity as commodity. The process of commodification is when objects, goods, services, and even ideas are transformed into tradable objects in a market place. A prominent feature of late capitalism is the creeping commodification of all aspects of life, including identity. Through media consumption and production, identity can also be consumed. The following sections in this chapter show some research-based examples of this process.

Naming in a networked society

Those who follow Latinx politics in the United States may have noticed the rise of the identifying term *Latinx*, which is generally used as a replacement for the terms *Latino* and *Latina* in English-speaking communities of Latinxs in the United States. The -*x* in *Latinx* symbolically eliminates the gendered language conventions of the Spanish language —the -*o* in *Latino* meaning masculinity, and the -*a* in *Latina* meaning femininity. I default to using the term *Latinx* in this book. As the next section shows, even the act of naming a population ties in uneasy and contentious politics.

According to Salinas and Lozano (2017), the term has found the most currency in higher educational institutions. The term *Latinx* was used online for the first time in 2004. Google Trends, as of 2019, indicates that the use of *Latinx* sharply rose in 2016 and has maintained common use since. In their article, Salinas and Lozano position *Latinx* as a term that is intersectional, meaning that it is inclusive of multiple identities. They claim that the term comes from indigenous populations in Mexico, which would be evidence of a flow of identity making coming from Latin America into the United States. This is noteworthy because scholars usually think of cultural flows emanating from the United States and imposing themselves onto the rest of the world.

The rise of the term *Latinx* has also, somewhat predictably, provoked a reaction against it. New articulations of identity are inherently destabilizing to cultural and political hierarchies. Thus, new terminology inspires intense reactions to its destabilizing power. For example, some critics have argued that it does not linguistically make sense, and others don't see a need to introduce another term naming Latinxs. While not a focus of this study, the term *Latinx* demonstrates the flexibility of Latinx identity. Its usage by specific ideological audiences, those with gender-neutral and leftist politics, further shows how political agendas are formed in networks, in this case academics and activists, and inserted via online interaction into the supposedly non-political practice of naming and categorizing people with heritage from Latin America in the United States.

Rinderle and Montoya (2008) set out to determine if there were salient demographic and/or cultural factors that influenced Latinxs' identification with one ethnic label. They found that the most salient, significant indicators of ethnic identification were class and language. Language might predict identification because language preference in this case probably approximates Americanization, or the extent to which a Latinx person feels closer to their U.S. or Latin American national identity. Those from higher classes also tend to identify with pan-ethnic terms. This might be because pan-ethnic labels were formed in elite, educated spaces. Higher-class Latinxs may also base their articulation of identity on their personal experiences in elite or cosmopolitan spaces.

The nexus of U.S. Latinx identity and mass media production is well established in the literature. Arias and Hellmueller (2016) surveyed the scholarship produced since the 1970s about U.S. Latinxs and the news media. They found that before the 1970s, there was almost no research conducted on Latinxs in the United States. Following the civil rights era, there was a movement to establish Mexican American/Chicano studies departments in U.S. universities. The development of these programs led to an increase in research on Latinxs and the news media. Research since then has primarily discussed four issues:

> (1) contextual factors and statistics of the growth of the Hispanic population in the United States; (2) the birth of the term "Hispanic" in comparison to the term of "Latino" as a demographic label and selfethnic identity labeling; (3) the pivotal role of media in popularizing the term "Hispanic between 1975 and 1994, and then news media framing on Hispanics between 1994 to 2015; and (4) attitudes toward Hispanics primed by news media that impact local immigration policies.
>
> (Arias, Hellmueller, 2016)

Each of these research strains has direct ties to the political discourse around Latinxs. The discussion of Latinxs as the "sleeping giant" arises out of the real notion that Latinxs are a growing sector of the population. The differences between the labels *Hispanic* and *Latino* are important distinctions since they evoke racial and class cleavages. The media also clearly plays a role in both the perception of Latinxs and in constructing, often via stereotyping, what a typical Latinx person is like. Finally, the rise of nativist anti-immigrant politics is partly associated with the presentation of Latinx immigrants as dangerous and law breaking.

Most of the theoretical sources I utilized in the previous chapter address at least one of these research issues listed by Arias and Hellmueller. The challenge for scholars of Latinxs and media is to move beyond the old production logic, which focuses on how cultural hegemony is extended through media by producers and passively received by audiences. For example, the authors rightly conclude their article by advocating for an image-based content analysis approach in research rather than an analysis of text, which is a vestige of the old media system. New media properties, such as YouTube and Instagram, are often text-light, meaning that the most important information is conveyed images, not words. This presents a challenge for scholars to analyze the media produced on those platforms.

There is some interesting research in this new media era. Chavez (2013) studied the Latinx television audience in a post-broadcast network era. His work focused on the development of mun2 (now rebranded as NBC Universo), a bilingual network targeting Latinx youth. Mun2 was a subsidiary of Comcast NBCUniversal and was like many of the national, regional, and local networks targeting Latinx audiences that emerged after the Telecommunications Act of 1996[2] (1027). Previously, the television marketplace for Spanish-language media was dominated by Univision and Telemundo. Mun2 was launched by NBCUniversal (NBCU) to capture what they saw as a new market of young Latinxs. When Comcast acquired NBCU, mun2 became a part of its parent company's asset portfolio. This also enabled further corporate synergy, which delivered content and advertisers to the network, effectively subsidizing mun2—an advantage not available to its competitors.

The main strategy around mun2 involved defining its audience as emblematic of the "new Latino." According to industry lingo, the "new Latino" is someone who is bilingual in English and Spanish, young, and tech savvy. This was understood in opposition to other Latinx audiences who primarily watch Univision and Telemundo. Those audiences were categorized as Spanish dominant and less socially mobile or cosmopolitan. Perhaps in the mind of the marketers, while the parents were watching *Sábado Gigante*, a popular Saturday program on Univison, their kids wanted to watch *Saturday Night Live* on their smartphones Monday afternoon. There is a real generational difference at play here too; second and third generations of U.S. Latinxs tend to use more English. The marketing discourse of the "new Latino" was further institutionalized by Nielsen when they released their report entitled *State of the Hispanic Consumer* in 2012. Almost ten years after the launch of mun2, the idea of the new Latinx audience is enmeshed even further in media production. This will be even more evident in the most recent research on U.S. Latinxs and online media.

The "New Latino" and online expression

A common rite of passage for Latinas in the United States is the *quinceañera*, a symbolic passage from girlhood to womanhood traditionally celebrated on a young girl's 15th birthday. While in Latin

America the term refers to the person, in the United States it has come to mean the party or celebration of her birthday. This is reflective of the transformation of the *quince* from a folk practice in Latin America to a performative one in the United States (González-Martin, 2016). In the United States, a small cottage industry of *quince* planners (similar to wedding planners) has emerged online via personal blog pages. These *blogueras* don't simply provide cultural knowledge and advice; they transform the *quince* into a performance where U.S. brands and products play a key role. For example, these online blogs often enter into sponsorship agreements with U.S. companies interested in multicultural marketing. According to González-Martin, the promotion of honey as the hot new food item for *quinces* is directly due to marketing by the National Honey Board indirectly promoted through the *quince* planners (57).

The production of *quince* information online in the U.S. context also exemplifies two features of online culture: remixing and configurability. González-Martin states that websites often deliberately call out some aspects of *quinces* as "outdated." They instead advocate for Latinas to make the celebration their own, in effect remixing the ritual with cultural capitalism. Latina youth thus navigate both tradition and U.S. consumerism via cultural expression, all with an eye on how the performance of the *quince* will be mediated via social media.

It should be clear that Latinx youth use social media to navigate their daily lives in multiple ways. Researchers have recently begun to appreciate how the modes of interaction among youth of color, especially Latinx youth, differ from those of majority populations. A dominant discourse in new media literature in the 2000s was focused on the so-called "digital divide" between different demographics of people (Pearce, Rice, 2013). Evidence now suggests that the digital divide is not as prevalent as it was a decade ago, but digital inequality exists in other ways (Van Deursen, Van Dijk, 2013). Most people in the United States have access to the Internet. It just so happens that, for Latinx youth, this access often comes through a mobile device (Brown, López, Lopez, 2016). It is worthwhile in this case to understand the differentiating practices, habits, and pathways constituting a divide when using mobile phones as the main point of access.

In terms of access, data from the Pew Hispanic Center indicate that the access divide is closing; Internet use among U.S. Latinxs increased by 14% between 2009 and 2012—from 64% to 78%. Increased mobile phone use, aided in part by more sophisticated feature innovation and affordable pricing, has played a pivotal role in closing the gap. Eighty-six percent of Latinxs report owning a cellphone, including 49% who report owning a smartphone. These levels are equivalent to—or higher in some cases—than other population groups. Among Latinxs, there remain some access divides, most of which are intuitive. Youth, higher income, and higher education levels positively correlate with access. For Latinxs who do not access the Internet, over two-thirds are foreign born. And even mobile phone access is not perfect. PCs and phones simply have different technological affordances. Imagine trying to write an essay for school on a mobile phone.

In this case, we can say that the Internet access divide has closed but the affordances divide is still an issue. Besides being unable to do things like write an essay on a phone, having Internet access restricted to digitally enclosed applications like Facebook and Instagram represents a limited experience. Young Latinxs may be getting a simplified, corporate-driven version of the Internet—one quite different from its promise of technological liberation. And the identity formed in such an environment will not be the same as if it were formed in a theoretically neutral public sphere.

Putting aside the access issue, there are other interesting trends and research into the unique pathways, practices, and skill sets being developed by Latinx youth. As outlined by the Digital Youth Project in *Hanging Out, Messing Around, and Geeking Out* (Mizuko, 2013), Latinx youth participate in digital culture just like other youth do according to danah boyd in her chapter on friendship (87–92). However, despite enjoying Internet access points through school and libraries, Latinx youth are challenged with uneven access. This presents issues when it comes to creative content production. Time constraints and access can interrupt artistic inspiration. Adult-led learning is also a barrier to creative production. In the same book from Mizuko, Tripp and Herr-Stephenson investigate how Latinx youth navigate limited or uneven access points to create content. Their ethnographic study focuses on Latinx youth who participate in a media production project through their schooling. While differentiating between adult-driven creative production and "fun, for themselves" creative production, these youth developed access strategies that involved smart use of school resources, the deployment of social capital to access friends' technologies, and the creative repurposing of other technology. Access at a superficial level seems consistent among Latinxs and other more privileged groups. However, access points are either highly policed by adults (at school, in the home) or technologically limited (older tech, lack of Internet connection), which presents important considerations around the question of digital divides.

Katz (2014) has theorized how Latinx youth serve as social brokers between their familial life and the community at large. Katz observes how children of immigrant families activate their unique socio-linguistic positioning in society to navigate mainstream society for their Spanish-dominant older relatives. In turn, they generate for themselves a unique skill set of intercultural communication. Particularly in this study, Katz investigated how youth brokered the health, financial, and administrative needs of their families by accessing community resources. For example, bilingual children were often relied upon to broker phone conversations when the caller did not speak Spanish. Katz reported that these calls were primarily translation brokerages. They were fairly common and usually adequately brokered. Issues arose when children were asked to broker printed media, as this often required high developmental barriers and competency in both languages. Brokering immigration forms, medical forms, and other documents laden with technical language often proved an anxiety-inducing cognitive load for Latinx youth. Katz concludes by suggesting that social brokering has negative effects on both maturation and educational pathways for Latinx youth, but potential positive effects on media literacy and intercultural dialogue.

Yosso (2005) also discusses how people on the margins have alternative sources of capital not traditionally recognized by dominant cultural institutions. She discusses how students of color bring different knowledges and means of navigating institutions from their backgrounds. She terms navigational capital as the ability to move through institutions like higher education with agency despite pervasive challenges. In a similar vein, Marchi (2016) investigated Latinx youth who read, analyze, and translate the news for their immigrant parents. She argued that their role as social brokers who interpret the news for their parents both flips the notion of the digital divide generationally and represents citizenship training. News interpretation among Latinx youth is a flipping of generational interaction: while in mainstream families the parents might educate their children about democracy and the news, in Latinx families it is the opposite. Latinx youth work as democratic chaperones to their elders living in a foreign land. For Marchi, this also doubles as their introduction to American democracy.

Navigating U.S. politics as a Latinx

What happens once networked Latinxs participate in U.S. politics? In other words, how do Latinxs in the United States navigate online spaces that intersect with established media and political institutions? Some recent research provides interesting findings. Political scientist Stokes-Brown (2018) provided a helpful breakdown of the role Latinxs played in the 2016 election. It should be noted that 1.5 million more Latinxs voted in the 2016 election than in the 2012 election. However, this large increase is mostly due to population growth and the maturation of a young population. The turnout rate of Latinxs dropped from 48% in 2012 to 47.6% in 2016. Leading up to the election, Latinx pundits observed that the Clinton campaign was doing little to mobilize Latinx voters. The pundits pointed to a poll showing that most Latinx voters did not think Trump was serious about his immigration policies. A sustained, Spanish-media effort from the Clinton campaign could have sharpened that issue, the pundits argued (Phillip, O'Keefe, 2016).

So, what did the Latinx vote do in 2016? It broke overwhelmingly for Hillary Clinton and the Democratic Party. However, this wasn't much of a surprise. What was surprising was that the rise of a nativist, heavily racialized candidate like Donald Trump did not drive more Latinxs to the polls or turn away the minority of Latinxs who vote Republican. In addition, Latinxs could not be relied upon by the Democratic Party as an electoral "firewall" against the GOP in places like Arizona and Florida. Stokes-Brown also provides evidence that in the 2016 election, Latinxs did not demonstrate the "group consciousness" political actors expected of them. She notes that the rhetoric against Mexicans by Donald Trump was not mobilizing for other nationalities of Latinxs. This is perhaps due to Trump singling out Mexicans first in his rhetoric. The Clinton campaign, according to Stokes-Brown, also made an error in 2016 by not selecting a Latinx vice presidential nominee. Stokes-Brown cites evidence that an ethnic candidate can be a mobilizing force for Latinxs.

The 2016 election is notable regarding not just how Latinxs voted but how Latinxs were talked about. Cisneros (2017) argues that the discourses around Latinxs during elections, particularly presidential elections, shape the broader political consciousness of Latinxs. In the 2016 election, Cisneros identified two dominant narratives around Latinxs. The first is the notion of the Latinx vote—or as it has been called by other scholars, the "sleeping giant" narrative. The second narrative is casting Latinxs as criminals, rapists, and socially deficient and in need of public assistance. Chavez (2013) has called this phenomenon the Latino threat narrative.

Interestingly, Cisneros sees the rhetoric around wooing the Latinx vote, typically used when discussing Republican candidates, as symbolic. He states that

> the gendered and sexualized nature of this metaphor of 'wooing' is important because part of what this narrative does is feminize this

'Latino vote' as already constituted and ready to be attracted by the right mix of appeals or the right (male) politician.

(516)

Latinxs in this frame are feminized by Democrats. Their feminization goes hand in hand with the passivity inherent in the sleeping giant narrative. By this logic, all it would take would be the right candidate to attract Latinx voters.

The threat narrative, however, does the opposite. The two narratives end up being two sides of the same coin. Latinxs are either a (masculine) threat that needs to be addressed violently or a fetishized (feminine) passive force that needs to be seduced. Both narratives share the same logic and "present Latinos as a singular and homogenous community, defined by common and essential demographic, linguistic, cultural, and ideological factors" (517). Both of these narratives were very common in the 2016 presidential campaign.

Anguiano (2016) identified a similar pattern in how Latinxs were presented as either a voting bloc to be wooed or a problematic community. She particularly takes issue with how the Democratic Party developed its outreach plan to Latinx voters. This famously included the Clinton campaign's release of a communication detailing "7 Ways Hillary Is Like Your Abuela." According to Anguiano, this is a perfect example of what has been termed "Hispandering." Hispandering usually refers to the superficial presentation of Latinx cultural signifiers (food, dress, etc.) as a discourse directed at Latinxs. Within the Latinx community online, there was a significant debate among those who tweeted #notmyabuela and those defending Clinton, including prominent figures like civil rights icon Dolores Huerta. Hostile language directed toward Latinxs gets the most academic and popular coverage. Hispandering, however, gets much less. The reaction against the Clinton campaign for their Hispandering also exemplifies how online networks can bring new voices to political debates. Further, the use of cultural signifiers into political marketing further exemplifies the transformation of identity into commodity.

Differences in online communication are also present in the interactions of members of Congress who are Latina and their constituents. Gershon (2008) studied the official website communications of female, African American, and Latinx members of Congress. While Congress is still overwhelmingly white and male, there has been a recent increase in diverse representation. For example, during the 2018 primary elections in Texas, voters elected two Latina candidates who ended up winning in the general elections. Gershon found that non-white and female members of Congress added a race and gender perspective to general policy issues. In effect, these members of Congress translated "neutral" policies into ones that had racialized or gendered implications. White or male members of Congress did not do this kind of contextualization.

Organizations that represent Latinxs in national policymaking also engage in a similar mode of communication. Smith and Abreu (2018) reviewed the memorandum of understanding (MOU) established between the Hispanic Leadership Organization and Comcast in relation to their proposed merger with NBCUniversal. The FCC used the language found in MOUs like this one Comcast negotiated to justify approving the merger. The MOU established that Comcast would increase content made for Latinxs, opportunities for Latinxs to create content, and leadership positions for Latinxs within the new corporate entity. In this case, advocacy groups were representing the interests of Latinxs. The advocacy groups argued for more representation in the conglomerated media landscape on behalf of Latinxs and in doing so, they adopted the neo-liberal language of increased consumer choice.

Smith and Abreu argue that the MOU was not honored and no significant changes around media representation of Latinxs occurred. The MOU also relied upon the common racialization of Latinxs discussed in Chapter 2. The authors state, "The categorization of Latina/o-owned and Latina/o-oriented media treats it merely as a form of capital in achieving diversity standards required by the FCC—or put more simply, 'a box to be checked'" (14). The Hispanic Leadership Organization (consciously or not) entered into an agreement with Comcast that further entrenched the racialized commodification of Latinxs in the United States. In addition, the racialization in the MOU enabled further consolidation of the media landscape under the guise of increasing diversity.

The research summarized in the previous sections considers how Latinxs in the United States navigate online spaces that intersect with established media and political institutions. Within these networks, Latinx identity is contested, reframed, updated, and commodified. It is not the case that identity homogenization is a simple, unidirectional process where elite actors and institutions shape Latinxs into perfect consumers of U.S. politics and ideology. Instead, Latinx subjects simultaneously receive essentialized narratives about themselves and selectively perform aspects in advantageous moments. Online, hybrid media networks enable the use of culture capital for Latinxs in ways not previously possible. These moments of performance vary by class and institutional circumstances, such as middle-class Latinas preforming *quince* culture online or Latinas in Congress giving intersectional context to policy issues. In summary, these works point to a post-modern system of racial performance. In this system, we preform our identity as Latinxs through media consumption and personalized new media. Culture then becomes a form of immaterial capital, or as I have said before—a commodity.

Notes

1 Defined as the merging of various previous separated technologies, indus-tries, and media onto one platform. Consumer electronics, telecommuni-cations, information technology, and media industries all were founded separately. Through corporate mergers (such as AT&T and Time Warner) and the Internet, media and technology have converged onto mobile phones and computers.

2 The Telecommunications Act of 1996 deregulated media ownership. After its passage, companies were allowed to own multiple stations and media properties in one market. This led to a rush of conglomeration and the seeking of new media markets, such as bilingual Latinx media.

References

Aldama, F. L. (2013). Multimediated Latinos in the twenty-first century: An introduction. In F. L. Aldama (Ed.), *Latinos and narrative media: Participation and portrayal* (pp. 1–31). New York, NY: Palgrave Macmillan.

Anguiano, C. A. (2016). Hostility and Hispandering in 2016: The demographic and discursive power of Latinx voters. *Women's Studies in Communication, 39*(4), 366–369. doi:10.1080/07491409.2016.1228385

Arias, S., & Hellmueller, L. (2016). Hispanics-and-Latinos and the U.S. media: New issues for future research. *Communication Research Trends, 35*(2), 4–21.

Brown, A., López, G., & Lopez, M. (2016, July 20). Hispanics and mobile access to the Internet. Retrieved November 02, 2018, from http://www.pewhispanic.org/2016/07/20/3-hispanics-and-mobile-access-to-the-internet/

Chadwick, A. (2013). *The hybrid media system: Politics and power.* Oxford, UK: Oxford University Press.

Chavez, C. A. (2013). Building a "new Latino" in the post-network era: Mun2 and the reconfiguration of the U.S. Latino audience. *International Journal of Communication, 7,* 1026–1045.

Cisneros, J. (2017). Racial presidentialities: Narratives of Latinxs in the 2016 campaign. *Rhetoric and Public Affairs, 20*(3), 511. doi:10.14321/rhet publaffa.20.3.0511

Dávila, A. M. (2012). *Latinos, Inc: The marketing and making of a people.* Berkeley, CA: University of California Press.

Van Deursen, A. J., & Van Dijk, J. A. (2013). The digital divide shifts to differences in usage. *New Media & Society, 16*(3), 507–526. doi:10.1177/1461444813487959

Gershon, S. A. (2008). Communicating female and minority interests online: A study of web site issue discussion among female, Latino, and African American members of congress. *The International Journal of Press/Politics, 13*(2), 120–140. doi:10.1177/1940161208315741

González-Martin, R. (2016). Digitizing cultural economies: 'Personalization' and U.S. quinceañera practice online. *Cultural Analysis, 15*(1), 57–77.

Katz, V. (2014). Children as brokers of their immigrant families' health-care connections. *Social Problems, 61*(2), 194–215. doi:10.1525/sp.2014.12026

Marchi, R. (2016). News translators: Latino immigrant youth, social media, and citizenship training. *Journalism & Mass Communication Quarterly, 94*(1), 189–212. doi:10.1177/1077699016637119

Mizuko, I. (2013). *Hanging out, messing around, and geeking out.* Cambridge, MA: MIT Press.

Mora, G. C. (2014). *Making Hispanics: How activists, bureaucrats, and media constructed a new American.* Chicago, IL: University of Chicago Press.

Pearce, K. E., & Rice, R. E. (2013). Digital divides from access to activities: Comparing mobile and personal computer Internet users. *Journal of Communication, 63*(4), 721–744. doi:10.1111/jcom.12045

Phillip, A., & O'Keefe, E. (2016, September 18). Among Democrats, deep concern about Clinton's hispanic strategy. Retrieved December 11, 2019, from https://www.washingtonpost.com/politics/among-democrats-deep-concern-about-clintons-hispanic-strategy/2016/09/18/38d3b99a-7c54-11e6-bd86-b7bbd53d2b5d_story.html

Rinderle, S., & Montoya, D. (2008). Hispanic/Latino identity labels: An examination of cultural values and personal experiences. *Howard Journal of Communications, 19*(2), 144–164. doi:10.1080/10646170801990953

Rodriguez, A. (1999). *Making Latino news: Race, language, class.* Thousand Oaks, CA: Sage.

Salinas, C., & Lozano, A. (2017). Mapping and recontextualizing the evolution of the term Latinx: An environmental scanning in higher education. *Journal of Latinos and Education,* 1–14. doi:10.1080/15348431.2017.1390464

Shirky, C. (2009). *Here comes everybody: The power of organizing without organizations.* New York, NY: Penguin.

Smith, J. A., & Abreu, R. (2018). MOU or an IOU? Latina/os and the racialization of media policy. *Ethnic and Racial Studies,* 1–19. doi:10.1080/014198 70.2018.1444187

Stokes-Brown, A. (2018). The Latino vote in the 2016 election—Myths and realities about the "Trump effect". In J. C. Lucas, C. J. Galdieri, & T. S. Sisco (Eds.), *Conventional wisdom, parties, and broken barriers in the 2016 election* (pp. 61–80). Lanham, MD: Lexington Books.

Winner, L. (1980). Do artifacts have politics? *Daedalus, 109*(1), 121–136.

Yosso, T. J. (2005). Whose culture has capital? A critical race theory discussion of community cultural wealth. *Race Ethnicity and Education, 8*(1), 69–91. doi:10.1080/1361332052000341006

4 Political mobilization in the post-modern digital era

If identity in the digital era has become a commodity to be traded, then a follow-up question might be—where and how? The answer I put forth in this chapter is that the realm of campaign political mobilization has become a new marketplace for identity trading. Advancements in digital technology, especially in the ability to track online behavior and subsequently analyze such behavior to craft bespoke political marketing, reify identity in the communication process. A straightforward example comes from Facebook. As an individual user, you can indicate your racial identity, hometown, relationship status, etc. on your profile. Based on your online behavior, such as likes of pages and posts, Facebook will then make a guess of your political identification for marketing purposes. Facebook's own guess of my political identification is "U.S. Liberal." In combination with other data Facebook offers, political advertisers may pay for ads targeting me in future elections based on this information.

In this chapter, I take a broader look at the contemporary mechanisms of political campaigning and organizing taking place in the hybrid and networked media ecology. These issues should be familiar to those with a background in political communication. This functions as a literature review covering topics such as data collection, data analytics, political advertisements online, and online campaigning. Many of these issues resonate with the 2016 and 2018 elections in the United States and the controversies that followed. These works focus on general, mass populations as opposed to U.S. Latinx populations, a general limitation of the field. The following chapters explore the connection to Latinx identity making in more detail based on my own research.

Digital politics—tools, opportunities, and vulnerabilities

Online digital media–based networks are simply changing how political campaigning and advocacy are being done. The early days of Web 2.0

were optimistically heralded as a new age for political participation (Shirky, 2009). Shirky argued the Internet allowed for horizontal organization of new groups outside traditional institutions, like government and the press. Small groups of citizens with very narrow and specific political interests could organize across geographic distances with ease. Shirky argued that the Internet dramatically lowered the barriers to group formation. Before the Internet, only large and resource-rich institutions could organize people consistently. In Shirky's words, "Newly capable groups are assembling, and they are working without the managerial imperative and outside the previous structures that bounded their effectiveness" (24). Shirky's work also provokes the question of how horizontal organizing develops group identity.

The 2010s saw several social movements which used digital tools to organize themselves. Hashtags, a feature of social media sites like twitter, enabled activists a space to organize themselves. Hashtag "activism," in other words, created strategic opportunities for groups like Black Lives Matter to organize themselves in new ways outside traditional power structures (Bonilla, Rosa, 2015). There was also a strain of techno-optimism around movements such as Occupy Wall Street and the Arab Spring even as they did not achieve their overall goals. Class and racial consciousness were raised by these movements.

Others are more pessimistic, especially in regard to the ability to selectively consume media that aligns with our partisan proclivities (Sunstein, 2007). Free expression is a vital component of deliberative democracy; the public sphere cannot exist without it. The selection of ideology-conforming news challenges the normative value of the public sphere. Referencing Habermas, Dahlgren (2005) argues:

> In schematic terms, a functioning public sphere is understood as a constellation of communicative spaces in society that permit the circulation of information, ideas, debates—ideally in an unfettered manner—and also the formation of political will (i.e., public opinion).
>
> (148)

The Internet, in this case, also enabled the selection and sorting of news that conformed to prejudices. The sorting of news sources may even lead to the breakdown of what is a person's or group's accepted notion of reality—a key foundation of identity.

Dahlgren later writes that the fragmented media landscape presents a challenge to the public sphere, which echoes Sunstein's concerns around siloed communicative spaces where there is little interaction with news and people who disagree. Dahlgren concludes by saying:

> The Internet is at the forefront of the evolving public sphere, and if the dispersion of public spheres generally is contributing to the already destabilized political communication system, specific counter public spheres on the Internet are also allowing engaged citizens to play a role in the development of new democratic politics.
>
> (160)

The Internet, in Dahlgren's view, allows for expanded free expression for those who are less likely to freely express their thoughts in the traditional unitary sphere. Those who argue for common experience and a general interest intermediary, like Sunstein, could just as rightfully argue that the Internet challenges democratic values.

Formal organizations play a key role in democracy. They represent citizens' concerns to systems of power. Hestres (2015) has discussed the differences between "Internet-mediated advocacy organizations" and more traditional "legacy" groups in climate advocacy (195–196). They differ in both how they conceptualize their theories of change (what will lead to action on climate change) and how their online strategies. Legacy groups, such as Greenpeace and Sierra Club, tend to focus on influencing elite opinion within policy and corporate institutions. As a result, their online strategy is more conservative. They do not ask too much of their followers—usually limited to signing petitions or donating. Newer Internet-based groups, however, have a much different theory of change—they believe in grander and transformation change though grassroots organizing. As a result, their online strategies focus on mobilizing supporters for more direct action and on the ground action. All organizations use digital tools—but "their strategic thinking on how to use these tools varies considerably between organizations" (207).

The past few years have shown that neither prediction about the fate of the Internet is totally true. New groups have found an outlet for their voices online, and powerful entities have co-opted the Internet for their own means. The past few years have seen an exponential rise in the development of new political campaign tools and practices regarding digital media. The following section details many of these innovations, their potential, and their vulnerabilities and their relationship to identity building.

Campaigns and political advertising online

Political campaigns, especially presidential campaigns, have changed dramatically. While Jamieson (1984) has argued that political campaigns have always responded to media such as newspapers by crafting messages for maximum media exposure, the emergence of television shifted how campaigns operated. Mediatization theory posits that media logic subsumes all other strategic concerns in campaigning. Digital media further shifts how campaigns are done now.

Kreiss (2016) conducted one of the most comprehensive studies of the development of technology-intensive campaigning since 2004. His primary conclusion is that the Democratic Party has invested more heavily in developing a technological edge in campaigning. To come to such a conclusion, he followed the careers of hundreds of party professionals as they moved in between campaigns, national party committees, boutique political firms focused on digital consultancy, and large tech companies. His approach is both historical and actor-network-based. He writes:

> The scholarly emphasis on the most visible aspects of contemporary campaigning—such as social media, email, online advertising, and websites—generally overlooks the ways that technology-intensive campaigning has reoriented parties and campaigns to the back-stage infrastructural technology, data, and analytics work that shapes all of electoral strategy and political communication from field campaigning and social media use to fundraising and media buying.
>
> (Kreiss 2016)

One of his main findings is that the Democratic Party basically "outsourced" innovation to competing firms to encourage innovation, while the GOP tried to innovate in-house and was less successful. In addition, Kreiss notes that how political "prototypes" of campaign technologies vary tremendously between parties and campaigns but also affect behavior. The digital architecture of each unique product shapes candidate and campaign interactions with the parties. For example, since the development of a national voter database by the Democratic National Committee (DNC) under the chairmanship of Howard Dean, candidates for office at all levels have used VoteBuilder (their system) to enrich the voter file with new information. Kreiss argues that third-party vendor databases are less useful when compared to this constantly updated database with near-universal democratic buy-in. Despite the labor poured into the system, the DNC ultimately retains the information therein. Kreiss concludes by arguing that this forms an "obligatory passage point" and reasserts the power of parties in the digital age.

Barnard and Kreiss expand on political advertising in a 2013 article. They define online political advertising as something that

> (1) campaigns or other political actors produce as discrete components of wider strategic communications efforts, (2) involves systematically evaluating progress toward defined goals through data, and (3) is conducted by a group of specialists recognized as such by their peers.

Political advertising is no longer just a means to convey a message by a campaign; it is also a means to gather data on which messages work and which do not.

In *Generation Digital* (2007), Montgomery writes about how political campaigns in 2004 used digital media to reach and engage youth. Following the disappointing youth turnout of the 2000 presidential election, a variety of organizations emerged to mobilize young people using a multifaceted strategy of pop culture and online media. Popular music was a starting point for mobilization, with record labels helping to fund groups like Rock the Vote. As Montgomery describes it, "The blending of music and politics was a powerful concoction that resonated with young people" (192). The juncture of music and politics also allowed for a wide variety of corporate interests to enter into youth mobilization, all hoping to inspire some brand loyalty among young, conscious consumers. The combination of celebrities and politics has further been sophisticated by the use of digital media and data from political campaigns.

Fulgoni, Lipsman, and Davidsen (2016) discuss the development of a program to deliver data-based political advertising. This program, which they call the "optimizer," helped campaigns micro-target voters using cable box systems. An optimizer is "a media-planning tool that used advanced demographic segmentation to find the combination of television shows that could reach the right audiences at the most attractive CPMs (cost per 1,000 ad impressions)" (241). The authors discuss how prior to the optimizer, campaigns would use the content of a television channel as a heuristic to divine the audience demographics. With the optimizer program, the Obama 2012 campaign was able to target audiences more efficiently and ended up spending less money on advertising than the rival Romney campaign in the 2012 U.S. presidential race.

Issenberg (2016) also discusses some of the data innovations that the Obama presidential campaign initiated. An interesting anecdote on data analytics is how predictive voter models were first used during the 2008 presidential campaign to make small-scale advertising purchases. This included buying ads on buses on specific routes in swing states that went through neighborhoods the campaign believed would be in favor of Obama. This anecdote exemplifies how analytics and data can be used to make unique and unconventional advertising decisions beyond TV and direct mail. Issenberg argues throughout the book that campaign strategists are always innovating to gain a competitive edge. The emergence of the Internet of Things (IoT)[1] will open a whole new playing field for political advertising.

Returning to Dahlgren, he notes that one of the main challenges to the integrity of the public sphere is "today's increased number of political advocates and 'political mediators,' including the massive growth in the professionalization of political communication, with experts, consultants, spin doctors, and so forth sometimes playing a more decisive role than journalists" (150). Professional political communicators are well skilled at creating simulacra of public engagement and free expression with political leaders. This is very much evident in political campaigning.

Stromer-Galley (2014) argues that campaigns operate under a "decidedly undemocratic view of *controlled interactivity,*" where campaigns use the genuine interaction of their supporters for their own ends—to gain power. She argues that the Internet and the communication tools surrounding it allow for "citizens [to be] like pawns on a chessboard: whom to move when to get the most strategic effect." She continues, "The power dynamic between campaigns and citizens, ultimately, is still hierarchical: candidates and their voices are valued over those of citizens" (18). Campaign professionals use the Internet to increase the feeling of democratic participation without giving up any of their power.

Voters as audience-identity constructions

So how do political actors conceptualize their voting audience? Hersh (2015) develops his perceived voter theoretical model in his book on data analysis and micro-targeting. He hypothesizes that campaigns use heuristics to categorize and develop messaging for voters. However, these heuristics are based on what data are publicly available— usually state electorate information. This model, he argues, contrasts with other research presuming that campaigns have a near-omniscient understanding of their constituencies. Instead, even the most advanced campaigns, such as Obama's reelection in 2012, are limited by campaign resources (time, volunteers, money, etc.) and the state-by-state variations of data.

Elected leaders have historically shaped policy on publicly collected data for their own campaign-related purposes. For example, collecting a voter's date of birth is argued as necessary to determine voter eligibility. Yet, this could also simply be represented in a binary output: 0 if the person is ineligible to vote (under age 18) or 1 if the person is eligible. The choice to record age is a policy decision and the result, in this example, is a publicly available database where campaigns can target people based on age. Differences between state databases also shape campaign decisions to target particular perceived voters. Campaigns target partisanship and race (two reliable predictors of someone's vote). How these categories are collected (or whether they are collected at all) vary state by state. For example, in Texas, voters do not register by party. However, the partisan primaries one votes in are recorded. Hersh basically finds that in states with partisanship, data campaigns target individuals, while in states without partisanship, data campaigns tend to target geographic areas where people of a similar partisanship are thought to live. Finally, Hersh is less convinced that commercial and social network data are useful to campaigns. First, he argues that campaigns are yet to decide about using many different variations of messaging to micro-target voters based on commercial data analysis. Second, he argues that while some cutting-edge campaigns (usually presidential) might experiment with commercial and social messaging (Obama in 2012, Cruz in 2016, etc.), the vast majority of campaigns (state, local, etc.) are yet to do so.

I am less convinced. In Soto-Vásquez (2017), I argue that the online activities common to everyday life—sharing on social media, commercial transactions, consuming news—should be understood though the economic frames of labor productivity and currency generation since they are now foundational to the political advertising ecosystem. I based my argument on short profiles I conducted of each major 2016 presidential campaign's data operation. I found that despite partisan and ideological difference, every major political campaign in 2016 had similar data collection policies in place. I wrote:

> Campaigns have long relied on unpaid labor to succeed. Volunteers are recruited and trained to reach voters and perform critical campaign functions. Digital campaigns are now tapping into the unpaid labor of online activity—by everyone, not just voters—to do their campaign outreach.
>
> (42)

The transition from Web 2.0 to Web 3.0, sometimes called the semantic web, means that all daily life will happen via the Internet. Web 3.0 is called the semantic web because those daily interactions create meaning through data—stories about our lives that can be bought and sold to external forces.

Part of the challenge in analyzing modern political communication in the United States is that the major political parties are not the tightly controlled hierarchical corporate entities they once were (Kreiss, 2016). In the current decentralized political moment—what Bimber (2011) calls the post-bureaucratic regime—political actors are creating new relations with new technologies at their disposal. Kreiss posits that in the long run, new relations will create new actors. For example, the Dean campaign in 2004 was the first campaign in recent U.S. politics to have a serious digital organizing component. Howard Dean, his campaign manager, Joe Trippi, and a staff of digital campaigners created new relations around the use of digital tools in campaigning. Eventually, Dean assumed the chairmanship of the Democratic Party and invested in a national digital plan for the party. New actors were created to manage databases, start digital consulting firms, and eventually elect Barack Obama in 2008.

But what about actual citizens and interest groups? Dave Karpf in *The MoveOn Effect* (2012) argues that the Internet has changed the way grassroots activism and advocacy groups maintain the relationship with their members. In the pre-Internet era, social movements had to invest a lot of resources in maintaining local civic chapters or mail-in membership. In contrast, Karpf notes the rise of new hybrid organizations that can operate on smaller budgets, quickly recruit new members based on the issue of the day. They can raise money online with less effort than a mail-out.

Karpf has also updated his work on advocacy groups and their use of analytical tools online in *Analytic Activism* (2016). Advocacy groups in the 2010s have become much more adept at using online tools to monitor their constituency groups online and respond to their political needs. Kreiss' and Karpf's work shows how political actors are adapting to the post-bureaucratic era of information distribution. These political data trends highlight the need for a deeper understanding of how identity works online. Is a person's identity something they firmly operationalize and then, by choosing how to use various online services, signal toward campaigns? Or is it the opposite? Do online campaigns look for digital traces that might signal that someone is Latinx and then impose that label upon them? Based simply on the previous literature, the answers are unclear at the moment.

Post-modern identity and politics

Pippa Norris argues that campaigns are operating in a "post-modern" campaign environment. She writes, "Politicians are essentially lagging behind technological and economic changes, and running hard to stay in place by adopting the techniques of political marketing in the struggle to cope with a more complex communication environment, rather than driving these developments" (Norris, 2000, 3–4). In this era, political marketers and advertisers have become co-equal to candidates in their role in driving campaigns. This frame begins to explain the conceptual problems regarding campaigns and identity just raised.

Post-modernism is a theory encompassing many fields of thought. In general, it refers to the period following the modern era and is usually understood in opposition to the assumptions of modernism. For example, where modernism upheld the scientific method and certainty, the post-modern mode of thought doubted the overarching narratives that sought to explain the world. In the realm of cultural products, post-modernism is marked by reliance on nostalgia, pastiche, diversity of representation, and hybridization of genres.

I have mentioned how the production in late capitalism in the post-modern context is focused on the cultivation of identity. Identity as a product in this context manifests in consumer goods, which can simultaneously be purchased and project a personal brand. For example, an urban, creative-class type might purchase fair-trade coffee and TOMS shoes to demonstrate their commitment to global environmental justice. Similarly, a rural, working-class person might purchase guns or a pick-up truck to demonstrate their commitment to rural traditionalism. In the post-modern context, politics becomes consumption.

Another feature of post-modern identity politics is that it is very flexible. A consumer can perform a certain affectation by consuming one type of product and then quickly shift to another brand to change up their personal brand. Latinxs in the United States do this often by consuming ethnic Latinx products (food, music, etc.) to demonstrate ethnic authenticity while staying true to mainstream U.S. cultural consumption (higher education, cars, etc.). They can also craft bespoke identities with niche brand consumption (fandom of Disney, for example) which then intersects with racial identity. Changes in personal brand can happen so quickly that the consumers themselves do not always notice them.

If post-modern politics is based on the performance of identity through the consumption of products, then it makes sense that political campaigns will base their political marketing on consumer data. Chester and Montgomery (2017) suggest that campaigns are becoming increasingly more sophisticated in their digital strategies. They say, "The digital media and marketing industry will continue its research and development efforts, with an intense focus on harnessing the capabilities of new technologies, such as artificial intelligence, virtual reality, and cognitive computing, for advertising purposes" (10). The dangerous implications for privacy are magnified by the fact that the U.S. legal system has very little protection of data compared to Europe.

The Obama campaigns drew data from commercial entities because they gave a good approximation for political values. The innovation of communication technologies that enable compression of distance between people and the time it takes to convey information also plays a critical role in the development of multiple political identities across many different groups of people. It is also important to note that in the post-modern era, one person can assume multiple identities concurrently and they may be incongruous.

From the field of political science, Abramowitz (2010) writes that the 2008 election exemplified the trends in the U.S. electorate toward identity polarization. The divide between party electorates showed increasing difference in region, religion, race, and ideology. Abramowitz argued that the Democratic Party was becoming the party of non-white voters. He also correctly predicted that the polarization of political parties according toward race could provoke a reactionary white nationalism among the right. The bemoaning of "identity politics" misses a larger point; all politics in the post-modern era is based on identity.

These trends from 2008 were evident in the highly racialized 2016 and 2018 campaigns. This increasing tying of political identity and racial identity is also part of the post-modern production of identity. The architecture of digital technologies online and the practices of data collection by campaigns are major accelerators of this trend. For example, the Trump campaign was able to specifically target online users with highly specific, and usually racialized, messages. In Florida, the Trump campaign was able to depress the turnout of African Americans by using social media dark posts highlighting the Clinton Foundation's work in Haiti (Grassegger, Krogerus, 2017). When a campaign decides to target one racial group in an area, it furthers the ties between partisan identity and racial identity. In addition, we can observe how contemporary political issues become racialized in the hyper-partisan political environment. Immigration as an issue becomes about racial anxiety toward Latinxs. Terrorism becomes about Muslims. Crime becomes about African Americans. Voter suppression moves beyond the polling place and registration to online, psychographic efforts to reduce someone's likelihood of voting.

Toward a "New Latino" hybrid

In the past three chapters, I have reviewed bodies of research directly related to the aim of this book. In Chapter 2, I synthesized a theoretical process of how U.S. Latinx identity is mediated by U.S. media institutions. There are generally three observable processes: the minimization of difference, denationalization, and racialization. These three processes do well to explain how Latinx identity was constructed in the late 20th century as marketers and media producers gradually realized the potential new market of Latinxs. However, the media system of today is much different than that of even a decade ago, never mind 40 years ago.

What is in place now is what Chadwick (2013) calls the hybrid media system. The hybrid system is a mix of old and new. This includes old and new media producers, old and new logics, and old and new audiences. The three processes I outlined in Chapter 2 were a result of the pre-hybrid system. In Chapter 3, I set out to review the most recent literature on the mechanisms of Latinx identity formation in a networked era. The lines between producer and consumer have been blurred, along with many other distinctions. Latinxs have acculturated to U.S. tastes and customs, especially in regard to the consumption of consumer products. Ethnic and folk practices from Latin America have transformed into multimedia spectacles where Latinx identity is performed. Latinx youth also have unprecedented access to a variety of tools for expression. A feature of the hybrid system is that it allows Latinx youth to select aspects of their traditional culture and remix them with more mainstream perspectives. This was the case in the literature on the labels youth have adopted, such as *Latinx*, or in spectacles such as *quinceañeras*.

Politics has also changed dramatically in the past two decades, as discussed in Chapter 4. The adoption and innovation of digital technologies by political campaigns and parties has brought up a whole host of issues. Both major U.S. political parties have developed sophisticated data operations. Campaigns since 2004 have grown accustomed to using personal data collected from their own websites and from other commercial sources to strategize and deliver advertising to voters. Even the smallest of campaigns, such as those for city council or the state house, can rent access to the parties' databases so they can target voters.

This change in political campaigning has shifted how candidates, campaigns, and parties see their constituencies as audiences. With the advent of digital politics, there has been a tendency to view voters less as citizens and more as consumers of a brand. The brands in politics are often candidate personalities, such as Barack Obama or Donald Trump, or party identification, such as Democratic or Republican. Political brands are also becoming closely tied to people's sense of identity. Political scientists call this phenomenon negative partisanship or polarization. A feature of negative partisanship is an intense distaste for the other political party. For example, Democrats may not agree with or even like their political leaders, but the GOP is so unacceptable to them that they will never cross party lines. The Clinton campaign in 2016 committed a critical misstep by attempting to appeal to Republican voters who they believed were disgusted by Donald Trump. In reality, voters receive so much negative information about the other side, delivered through traditional and digital media, that split-ticket voting is truly a relic of the past.

The tying of identity and politics is best described, as Norris noted, as post-modern politics. People vote and mobilize themselves according to how they conceptualize their identity. Applying rational modernity to politics is a gross oversight. Few people vote on which issues make the most sense to them. Voters are not rational actors. Voters elect those leaders who confirm their worldview. Political advertising based on personal data has accelerated these trends as well. Groups like Cambridge Analytica can profile the fears and prejudices of a community and deliver a perfectly targeted message. These messages can then mobilize voters based on appealing to powerful emotions, such as fear of others.

What does all this mean for the relationship between established political groups and U.S. Latinxs? Unfortunately, my review of the literature shows that there is little research in this area. Contemporary literature of Latinxs is just now considering digital media and its identity-shaping role. Studies on contemporary political campaigns focus on broad mainstream audiences and often leave out Latinxs. This gap in the literature informs the larger research questions I ask in this book. I am focused on how Latinx advocacy groups use digital media to mobilize voters and, as a byproduct, make assumptions about identity that are then encoded into digital apparatuses. In my research methodology, I also drew on some of the issues raised by the literature—such as whom do groups view as their audience and how do they listen to them?—to articulate the questions I asked my interview subjects. The aim of the following three chapters will be to bridge this gap and consider how U.S. Latinx political identity is shaped by organizational communication practices.

Note

1 Generally understood as a network of devices, vehicles, appliances, and other consumer goods connected to the Internet.

References

Abramowitz, A. I. (2010). Transformation and polarization: The 2008 presidential election and the new American electorate. *Electoral Studies, 29*(4), 594–603. doi:10.1016/j.electstud.2010.04.006

Barnard, L., & Kreiss, D. (2013). A research agenda for online political advertising: Surveying campaign practices, 2000–2012. *International Journal of Communication, 7*, 2046–2066.

Bimber, B. A. (2011). *Information and American democracy: Technology in the evolution of political power.* Cambridge, UK: Cambridge University Press.

Bonilla, Y., & Rosa, J. (2015). #Ferguson: Digital protest, hashtag ethnography, and the racial politics of social media in the United States. *American Ethnologist, 42*(1), 4–17. doi:10.1111/amet.12112

Chadwick, A. (2013). *The hybrid media system: Politics and power.* Oxford, UK: Oxford University Press.

Chester, J., & Montgomery, K. C. (2017). The role of digital marketing in political campaigns. *Internet Policy Review, 6*(4), 1–20.

Dahlgren, P. (2005). The Internet, public spheres, and political communication: Dispersion and deliberation. *Political Communication, 22*(2), 147–162. doi:10.1080/10584600590933160

Fulgoni, G. M., Lipsman, A., & Davidsen, C. (2016). The power of political advertising: Lessons for practitioners how data analytics, social media, and creative strategies shape U.S. presidential election campaigns. *Journal of Advertising Research, 56*(3), 239. doi:10.2501/jar-2016-034

Grassegger, H., & Krogerus, M. (2017, January 28). The data that turned the world upside down. Retrieved November 02, 2018, from https://mother board.vice.com/en_us/article/mg9vvn/how-our-likes-helped-trump-win

Hersh, E. D. (2015). *Hacking the electorate: How campaigns perceive voters.* Cambridge, UK: Cambridge University Press.

Hestres, L. E. (2015). Climate change advocacy online: Theories of change, target audiences, and online strategy. *Environmental Politics, 24*(2), 193–211. doi:10.1080/09644016.2015.992600

Issenberg, S. (2016). *The victory lab: The secret science of winning campaigns.* New York, NY: Broadway Books.

Jamieson, K. H. (1984). *Packaging the presidency: A history and criticism of presidential campaign advertising.* New York, NY: Oxford University Press.

Karpf, D. (2012). *The MoveOn effect: The unexpected transformation of American political advocacy.* Oxford, UK: Oxford University Press.

Karpf, D. (2016). *Analytic activism: Digital listening and the new political strategy.* Oxford, UK: Oxford University Press.

Kreiss, D. (2016). *Prototype politics: Technology-intense campaigning and the data of democracy.* Oxford, UK: Oxford University Press.

62   *Digital political mobilization*

Montgomery, K. C. (2007). *Generation digital: Politics, commerce, and childhood in the age of the Internet.* Cambridge, MA: MIT Press.

Norris, P. (2000). *A virtuous circle: Political communications in postindustrial societies.* Cambridge, UK: Cambridge University Press.

Shirky, C. (2009). *Here comes everybody: The power of organizing without organizations.* New York, NY: Penguin.

Soto-Vásquez, A. D. (2017). Reconceptualizing digital privacy: Examining two alternatives in the 2016 presidential election. *The Journal of Communication and Media Studies, 2*(2), 33–45. doi:10.18848/2470-9247/cgp/v02i02/33-45

Stromer-Galley, J. (2014). *Presidential campaigning in the Internet age.* New York, NY: Oxford University Press.

Sunstein, C. R. (2007). Neither Hayek nor Habermas. *Public Choice, 134*(1–2), 87–95. doi:10.1007/s11127-007-9202-9

5 The professional political class of U.S. Latinxs

A few weeks before the 2016 presidential election, on an unseasonably warm October day, the Barack Obama administration held a White House Latinx policy summit in the Eisenhower Executive Office Building. Like many young and underpaid residents of Washington, D.C., I had honed my ability to get into events with important people with free food. I secured my invitation days before the event through a friendly connection. Unfortunately, there was no free food. What I observed at this policy summit would inform the early stages of my book research and how I specifically frame the research question I address in this chapter.

The 2016 White House Latinx policy summit gathered together more than 40 national Latinx organizations, under the banner of the National Hispanic Leadership Agenda (NHLA). The NHLA is an umbrella organization of national Latinx groups. The event was designed partly to bring together actors within the organization and develop new networks but also to extol the policy gains made during the Obama administration and point the way forward in the next administration. Discussion during the event focused on the gains made for Latinxs as a result of the Affordable Care Act and other policies.

The event was purposely non-partisan and avoided any discussion of the election or hypothesized results. The reason for a non-partisan event, as many participants repeatedly said, was the Hatch Act—a law preventing federal employee participation in elections. Nonprofits also want to avoid engaging in overtly partisan events. Given that the event was occurring at the White House, the organizers took precautions to avoid the semblance of favoring a specific outcome of the election. Nevertheless, there were strong winks and nods exchanged between attendees. One advocate from a Latinx organization said, "We will happily work with the next president is—*whoever she may be*" [emphasis mine].

The event kicked off with the president of the Mexican American Legal Defense and Educational Fund (MALDEF), Thomas Saenz, introducing Housing and Urban Development (HUD) Secretary Julián Castro. Castro is the former mayor of San Antonio, Texas and was a 2020 Presidential candidate. There was some speculation in early 2016 that this young, Harvard- and Stanford-educated Latinx could be selected as Hillary Clinton's running mate. In early 2016, there was an unofficial campaign by D.C. Latinxs to encourage the Clinton campaign to pick Castro as her running mate. They argued that Castro would inspire Latinxs to turn out in favor of Clinton. The Clinton campaign believed that Latinxs would turn out regardless, due to Trump's rhetoric, and decided that they should pick a southern white moderate politician who could potentially peel off some disaffected Republican voters.

Despite the failure at convincing the campaign to select a Latinx running mate, there was still plenty of optimism about the likely Clinton administration. An Obama administration political appointee told me that before the election, many staffers were updating their resumes, ready to apply for jobs or promotions in the new administration. The futures of Castro and many of the other figures present at the policy summit would drastically change over the course of the next months in the Trump administration. The surprising result of the 2016 election would scramble the leadership of the Washington, D.C., Latinx political class and challenge many of my own assumptions about Latinx politics.

The issues facing U.S. Latinx political leadership in the Trump era are about mobilizing a community under attack, developing a compelling message, and using the technologies of the time to do so. I address these issues with an academic approach, using the frames of homogenization, Americanization, and denationalization, along with the affordances of new media to discuss the findings.

In this chapter, I discuss the results of a multiyear study of national Latinx organizations in the United States, my interactions with organizational actors and activists, and extensive notes gathered from attending multiple events across the country. As I will discuss in detail, I found that the class background of organizational actors shapes much of their discourse toward idealizing of the American dream and general avoidance of transformational politics. In this chapter specifically, I set out to answer the following research question: *How do organizations strategically construct an essentialistic discourse of U.S. Latinx identity?* In previous chapters, I discussed how Latinx identity was generally mediated in the mass media as well as how identity making is shifting in a digital, hybrid media system.

Within this research question, there are two key sub-questions that will structure the findings presented in this chapter. First, *how do stakeholders within organizations conceptualize their audience and market position?* In this question, I investigate how actors within organizations generate knowledge, formulate heuristics about their audience, and understand their influence. From this perspective, I tried to uncover how personalities and unique backgrounds influence the projection of identity and strategy. The second related sub-question is as follows: *How do stakeholder organizations use national conferences to shape their discourse for constituents?* In this question, I look at the use of national conferences to create networks and set agendas. In the subsequent chapters, I address the adoption and use of digital technology in depth and media portrayal, while this chapter is focused on the interpersonal.

I approach each question through the framework laid out in the preceding chapters. So, for example, how do stakeholders conceptualize their audience and market position in terms of *denationalization* or *racialization?* Later in this section, I also address other themes, primarily the role of the 2016 election. As a reminder, the data presented in this chapter is drawn from extensive interviews and public observations made in 2017 and 2018. For a more detailed discussion of the methodology, refer to Chapter 1.

Minimization of difference

I have defined the minimization of difference as a process in U.S. Latinx identity making where the difference highly present in Latin America, such as racial, ethnic, and physical characteristics, is ignored or generalized in U.S. media. Scholars of mass media have observed homogenization. Difference in online media is presented with greater complexity. Online media has the tendency to both entrench racial and ethnic identity and deconstruct it. This complex, even contradictory tendency played out in the research conducted.

Two primary themes of homogenization emerged. First, the subjects I observed and interacted with all occupy a specific class of political professionals. Their class position is an important part of the work they do, so I detail some of their backgrounds in this section. Second, the class position of the actors I observed also transforms how they conceptualize identity. Homogenization of Latinxs has traditionally come from mass media production, as in the stereotypes and caricatures presented in advertisements and other forms of media. There has recently been a shift, however. Identity is also created in networked communication among elite actors who have internalized certain notions about Latinx people. In the second section, I detail how actors use their personal and professional networks as influences in their framing of identity.

The first marker of class identity that differentiates the interview subjects from the general population of Latinxs in the United States is their education. While according to Pew only 15% of Latinxs aged 25–29 have a college degree (Krogstad, 2016), all of my interview subjects held college degrees. They were also distinguished by the type of schools they went to; most went to elite private schools, such as Georgetown University, George Washington University, American University, Boston College, or selective public schools, such as the University of Texas. This contrasts with most other Latinxs, who, if they do attend college, attend non-selective, public, two-year colleges.

In his 1976 book *The Culture of Professionalism*, historian Burton J. Blesdstein describes how professionalism emerged in the United States as a form of social status. Since the United States has no aristocracy, he theorizes that becoming a professional was a way to attain social status. It was especially powerful since this status could be defended as earned on merit instead of the chance of birth. Bledstein argues that the university in the 20th century became the prime institution for the development of the professional class. Credentialism, the belief that someone's academic or other formalized credentials measure intelligence or their ability to do a job, became rampant. For many Latinxs hoping to enter the middle class and seek economic stability, higher education is often the only pathway, since familial social capital is limited. The Civil Rights era opened up educational pathways for Latinxs. Thus, many middle-class Latinxs have internalized the logic of professionalization. In turn, many well-educated Latinxs struggle with the disjuncture between their professional culture and the culture of their upbringing.

The subjects I interviewed occupy this same professional class position. For example, my study of their LinkedIn profiles revealed that many came to their positions working for Latinx advocacy groups through corporate businesses or political organizing with major campaigns, especially the Obama and Clinton presidential campaigns. Perez and Murray (2016) found a similar professional class orientation of Latinx advocacy board members, with most board members holding elite educations and corporate ties. They write:

> The ethnic elites who sit on the boards of these nonprofits occupy these positions in large part because of their ties to nonethnic elite networks. Because of their elite affiliations, the board members of ethnic organizations signal legitimacy and adherence to corporate and professional norms.

(134)

This pattern is reflected in the professional staff of the advocacy groups I interviewed.

The last marker of class identity was the cities they lived in. All subjects lived in either Washington, D.C., or Austin, TX. Both are destination cities where young people move to advance their careers. While I did not interview anyone in Los Angeles, CA, where a few Latinx organizations are headquartered, Los Angeles is also experiencing a similar influx of young professionals from around the country. These cities are prime examples of cosmopolitan areas (Keith, 2005) where ethnic diversity is highly present. These cities have unique cultural practices. Food culture (including diverse foods), public transportation use, fewer families, and more unmarried young adults make cities different from the rest of the country. Austin, D.C., and LA have all seen a recent dramatic rise of gentrification over the last several years as well. Longtime residents have been pushed out as new residents, often well-educated young professionals, move in.

How does their class position affect their understanding of the Latinx population they serve? The first mechanism is subtle but important. Elite Latinx professionals in politics will often extend their experiences and background to make assumptions about their constituencies. When I asked a staffer to name some barriers to Latinxs voting, she responded by saying, "A lot of young Latinx voters are like me. They have moved around a lot in their life for school and work, so it is hard to register them to vote at one address." While it may be the case that young professionals who attended elite universities have moved from their hometowns to places like Austin and D.C., this is a not a common experience for most Latinxs in the United States. According to a study from the UCLA Higher Education Research Institute, a little more than half of Latinx college freshmen go to a four-year school more than 50 miles away from their families.

The second, and more common, feature to all interview participants is their belief in the mythology of the American Dream. Since many have "made it" as successful professionals through higher education, their politics are often focused on incremental, progressive change. Instead of proposing radical change, they often advocate for working within the system and increasing access to traditional institutions, such as higher education. For example, many subjects described the sacrifices their parents made in order for them to do what they do now. The mythology of the American Dream also surfaces in their digital media, which I will cover in the next chapter.

Finally, their sense of the important issues facing Latinxs in the United States is highly influenced by the sources of information they consume. I asked all interview subjects how they gather information about their audiences. None of the responses were highly technical. Instead, they use their organizational and personal Twitter accounts as networks of information. One subject noted, "I look at my Twitter feed to see what is happening. I read what my right-wing and left-wing friends are saying and figure our agenda has to be somewhere in the middle." The issue that emerges from this heuristic research practice is that the networks of followers Latinx professionals access tend to be sorted by educational and class background. Perez and Murray (2016) found that ethnic elites rely not only upon their networks of fellow ethnic elites but also upon non-ethnic elite networks associated with corporate power. This process is similar to the classic communication theory of agenda setting, where news and policy makers set the terms for what is a legitimate political issue and what is not. Elite networks tend to be ultimately conservative in the grand scheme of politics, as radical change would disrupt their position in a hierarchical society.

These combined trends demonstrate that Latinx identity formation doesn't happen just in the traditional way we imagine through mass media (what a Neo-Marxist might call homogenizing media production); it also occurs in the networked articulation of elite Latinxs. When I asked one subject what they imagine their audience as a national Latinx advocacy group to be, they responded by saying, "I imagine people like my parents, hardworking and decent people." At the same time, interview subjects also expressed strong views on external forces that homogenize the experience of U.S. Latinxs. All expressed a strong distaste toward the Trump administration, his supporters, and his nativist rhetoric. They objected to all Latinxs being cast as rapists or "bad hombres," as the President has famously said several times.

Beyond nativist rhetoric, the subjects were also frustrated with those, even allies, who approach Latinxs as a monolithic community. For example, one individual I met at a conference said that they were tired of allies they work with assuming all Latinxs are poor, uneducated, and/or immigrants. They noted that many of their organizations have local chapters that provide diversity within their organizations. A staffer from LULAC noted that their organizational structure is made up of locals, with everyone from college chapters to LGBTQ-focused chapters exerting pressure upon the national organization. The dynamic between the local and the national, especially with LULAC and Voto Latino, exemplified my subject's characterization of their work as influential nodes in a larger network. They receive, collect, and interpret information about their audience and then transmit messages to important actors and constituencies in the network.

To summarize, actors with Latinx advocacy organizations engage in the homogenization of Latinxs through a process that differs from mainstream media production. This is an important departure from how Latinx homogenization has been theorized in the past. Dávila (2012) wrote that the innovators of Latinx marketing imposed their own class status onto the characteristics of the Latinx market they shared with potential customers. In other words, since the early Cuban American marketers were professionals who had housewives, were religiously Catholic, and were socially conservative, they extended those characteristics to all Latinxs in the United States. They have since stuck. Professional Latinx advocates are a largely homogenous group themselves and occupy a professional class position with elite educations. They are distinct from activists. Actors within Latinx advocacy groups use their online networks as a means of deriving information and news about their Latinx audiences. They also substitute their experiences for the experiences of Latinx audiences at large.

This is all occurring in a hybrid media environment. Professional Latinxs constructing identity in a hybrid media environment moves identity formation from a unidirectional process of media homogenization to the one where actors form identity in digital social networks. They do, however, trouble the homogenization they feel is imposed on Latinxs by external forces and believe that there is tremendous diversity across localities. In sum, difference is minimized since the understanding of the Latinx audience is conceptualized by a select few—in this case, the Latinx professional political class.

Denationalization

The second major process of Latinx identity formation in the United States is denationalization. Denationalization is a process in which the U.S. American identity of Latinxs is emphasized, while the national identities of their origin countries are deemphasized. As mentioned earlier, the vast majority of Latinxs in the United States prefer to identify by their national origin, thinking of themselves as Mexican or Puerto Rican before Latinx. In this section, I will discuss several themes from my observations of national conferences. First, the symbolic renationalization of Latinxs as U.S. Americans, the close association with U.S. American symbology, and the discursive tying of military service to Latinx identity. Second, I discuss how my interview subjects and rhetoric at conferences have elevated Dreamers as a special constituency of Latinxs for political action to exemplify the U.S. Americanness of Latinxs. Finally, I discuss the symbolic nationalization of Latinxs as full-fledged U.S. American consumers of brands and products at conferences.

Denationalization as a process seems similar to assimilation but is different in a key way. Used colloquially, the term *assimilation* refers to how minority groups gradually adopt the cultural practices of the majority culture in which they live. Immigrants to the United States have historically assimilated to U.S. American culture, although recent social movements around multiculturalism have encouraged new immigrant groups to maintain a stronger degree of cultural identity from their origin countries. Denationalization is different in that it is a discursive practice, rather than a cultural trend. Denationalization is used as a discursive strategy to describe people; it is not done by the population themselves.

At national conferences, the close association with U.S. American values and symbols is highly present. Every national conference that I attended began, usually at the first major plenary or keynote address, with the national anthem, the Pledge of Allegiance, and either an honor guard procession or flag symbology. At the LULAC conference in 2017, the national anthem was performed by a musician using an accordion in the style of regionally popular Tejano music. As mentioned in Chapter 2, LULAC is distinguished by its history of advocating for the rights of Latinxs by emphasizing their patriotism and, in some cases, whiteness. Military service is also highlighted as an important aspect of U.S. American identity. At the NALEO conference, participants who had served in the military were asked to stand and be recognized by branch of the military.

Democratic traditions and participation are also held up as the highest possible action by Latinx youth. They are asked to vote, get involved in civic life, and accept their role as citizens of the country. This rhetoric often takes a guilty, self-flagellating tone. At the Voto Latino conference in late 2017, actor Wilmer Valderrama said that Latinxs have let each other down by not voting at the level they should be. Even Latinxs who are not citizens and therefore cannot vote are asked to get civically involved through organizing.

What is not present? Any critique of U.S. imperialism or the history of oppression of Latinxs in the country. Speakers will avoid coming across as anti-American, instead placing blame on bad politics and bad actors. They often emphasize the fundamental goodness of the country. This is reinforced by the speakers who are invited to the conferences. Reviewing the programs of all the conferences I attended over the course of 2017, I found that most speakers came from politics or policymaking. Another significant group came from business or corporate positions. Few came from nonprofit positions, and even fewer came from activist backgrounds.

The denationalizing of Latinxs and emphasis on U.S. American identity finds the perfect rhetorical subject in the Dreamer. Dreamers are a group of young people who are distinguished by a few factors. First, they were brought into the United States by their parents and, in most cases, lack legal authorization to live in the country. Second, despite their citizenship status, Dreamers are either in college or recently graduated. Finally, Dreamers have become the focal point for immigration reformers. The failure to pass a legislative fix for DACA in early 2018 became a controversial issue among Latinx advocacy groups.

The framing around Dreamers from Latinx advocacy groups makes it clear why Dreamers are elevated to the national discourse around immigration. Dreamers are often framed as "American in all regards, except in legal status." They end up being the "perfect" immigrants, reflecting the values of a meritocratic, professionalized economy. They are well educated, contributors to the economy, and moral members of society. Some scholars have noted that this framing ends up casting the Dreamer as the "good, worthy immigrant" and other immigrants as less worthy (Chuang, Roemer 2014).

This framing was highly present at the official fora I observed. After observing the various conferences, one could walk away assuming that all undocumented immigrants are in college and on the track to successful professional careers. One conference speaker summarized it well, stating that Dreamers are the best example of why immigrants "make America great." Speakers hold up Dreamers when arguing with the rhetoric of nativist politicians, saying that they represent Latinxs' belief in the American Dream. This sentiment is not entirely unfounded. Polls by Pew and other sources have found that more than half of Latinxs in the United States believe that hard work will lead to economic security. This belief in the American Dream is much less widely held by white and black Americans (Smith, 2017).

The final theme is how closely Latinx advocacy groups align themselves with corporations. The historical trend of neoliberalism severed the distinction between the market and every other aspect including society, education, government, dating, etc. In neoliberalism, the market is literally everywhere. For Latinx advocacy organizations, this primarily includes the sponsorship of conferences and the funding of the work they do. This was not always the case for Latinx groups, according to Perez and Murray (2016). In the 1970s, many Latinx organizations, especially those based in Texas and California, were fairly radical in their politics and very litigious. However, their radical perspective was soon challenged by financial and personnel issues. In exchange for corporate funding, especially funneled through the Ford Foundation, Latinx advocacy groups were forced to move to D.C. and professionalize their approach to community work.

At the conferences, corporations exerted a unique kind of influence I had not previously encountered in the literature. Stories of success, such as an immigrant Latina working multiple jobs to provide for her family, were connected to the goodness of corporations providing opportunities for Latinxs to move up from entry-level jobs to middle management. Before the keynotes or plenaries of major conferences, a worker who was emblematic of this success represented their corporate sponsor by speaking to the audience. Their stories of achieving the American Dream, in their words, were possible though corporations, diversity initiatives, and their hard work. What is the effect of such speeches? First, it absolves corporations of their role in harming Latinxs in the United States. Wal-Mart is the largest employer of Latinxs in the United States, and a major sponsor of many national Latinx advocacy organizations. The company is also notorious for worker abuse and low employee wages. Second, the prominence of corporations in these Latinx spaces limits the range of political and policy options up for debate. For example, at the LULAC conference in San Antonio, there was a panel on the topic of Internet privacy and Latinxs. It also happened to be sponsored by Charter Communications (the parent company of Spectrum, a major Internet service provider) and Comcast NBCUniversal. The conversation inside the room on the panel avoided a critique of Internet monopolies and privacy policies. Instead, the discussion focused entirely on corporate efforts to increase the tech-savvy Latinxs though community technology sources. In other words, the onus for protection was put on the consumer instead of on the company. Political change was off the table.

To summarize, the denationalization of Latinxs in the United States is a process in which the national identity of Latin American heritage is shed and U.S. American identity is emphasized. It is a rhetorical strategy to show the Americanness of Latinxs as a means to secure rights. The national conferences observed in my study did not focus on deemphasizing sending country national identity. They instead focused on articulating the Americanness of Latinxs in unique ways. First, the symbols and practices of U.S. national identity were strongly emphasized at each conference. In some cases, there was a Latinx flavor given to the practices, such as performing the national anthem with an accordion in San Antonio. The military service of Latinxs was also highly emphasized. Second, Dreamers were rhetorically framed as the good, worthy immigrants who are "American in every respect but their documentation." Finally, the presence of U.S. American corporations creates a unique narrative in which the achievement of the American Dream by Latinxs is directly tied to the diversity initiatives of the companies and the hard work of Latinxs. In all, the denationalization of Latinxs in the United States in this case tracked closer to Americanization. The ultimate goal of denationalization, as presented by Latinx advocacy organizations, is to frame Latinxs as legitimate members of U.S. society and worthy recipients of full citizenship.

Racialization

Racialization in the United States is the final process outlined as a force shaping contemporary Latinx identity. In Latin America, the effects of Spanish and Portuguese colonialism created a highly racialized and stratified society based on the mixture of European, African, and indigenous people. This varies from place to place as well. The Dominican Republic had a large importation of African slaves to work on plantations. Argentina has a very ethnically European population due to receiving many immigrants from Italy and Spain after World Wars I and II. It is also important not to historicize indigenous communities in Latin American as a feature of the past. Indigenous people live and struggle in liminal spaces throughout Latin America. For example, over six million ethnically Mayan people live in southern Mexico and Central America. Depending upon the mixture of indigenous, African, and/or European ancestries, a person could be placed into racial categories such as mestizo or mulatto in the Latin American racial system. Historically, these categories closely aligned with the power hierarchy in Latin America. Whites held the most power (and still do), mestizos occupied a buffer right under the white elite, and everyone else fell in line at the bottom. This triracial system is a feature of Latin American racial politics (Bonilla-Silva, 2010) and a concept I will return to later.

Once Latinx identity is discursively formed in the United States, the complex racial categories and politics of Latin America are glazed over. Instead, Latinxs in the United States are racialized as a corporate, racial group themselves. They are framed as different from white and black Americans in the United States, two groups that have their own unique racial history in the country. My interviews and observations revealed some of the ways that racialization works in the United States. First, the interview subjects rhetorically placed Latinxs within a broader people of color (POC) coalition. Second, the conferences I observed placed a heavy emphasis on the position of Mexican Americans in the Latinx community. In effect, Mexican Americans and their stories were centered in discourse. The idea of Mexican hegemony in Latinx politics is important here. Finally, there was a little discussion of racial difference among Latinxs themselves, even as issues around Afro-Latinxs and other groups have gained more traction.

A staffer noted that the general neglect of the Trump administration toward Latinx groups has encouraged Latinx groups to strengthen alliances with other ethnic groups. They noted that the CHC has begun to work more closely with the Congressional Black Caucus (CBC) and the Congressional Asian Pacific American Caucus (CAPAC) to advance legislative goals and defend their constituencies from harmful policies. Other groups, like Voto Latino and NALEO, also stressed the need to build partnerships and learn from communities like the African American community. This is an example of placing Latinxs alongside other traditional ethnic minority groups (African American, Asian American) into what is referred to as a coalition of POC. The term *people of color* (POC) is predominantly used in the United States to describe all non-white people. The placement of Latinxs into the POC coalition further racializes them as a distinct racial group in the national discourse. In addition, a staffer noted that the need for alliances among other POC groups was based on the weakening of the White House as a central node for organizing and coordinating in D.C. During the Obama administration, a special office existed in the White House that would coordinate policy and legislative plans with Latinx advocacy groups. The Trump administration has deemphasized that office and, as a result, Latinx organizations have had to rebuild their own information sharing networks from scratch.

All of the conferences in 2017 were held in the Southwest. Phoenix, Arizona, is a popular conference location—hosting UnidosUS in 2017, along with LULAC and NALEO both in 2018. The Southwest is notable because among Latinxs, Mexicans and Mexican Americans compose the largest sub-group. The southwestern United States is also where the vast majority of Mexican Americans live and where political action by Mexican Americans has been centered. San Antonio, where LULAC held its 2017 annual convention, is an especially important node in the organizing history of Mexican American advocacy groups. LULAC, the American GI Forum, and the Southwest Voter Registration Education Project (SVREP) all trace important founding legacies to San Antonio. In effect, the placing of conventions in the Southwest centers the experiences of Mexican Americans in the Latinx narrative. This centering of Mexican Americans takes a few forms. Discourse at conferences creates a narrative of the struggle for full civil rights for the broader Latinx community through the struggles of Mexican Americans in the 20th century. Mexican American leaders like Cesar Chavez and Dolores Huerta are idolized. Speakers at the conference also tend to be Mexican American, so the personal narratives shared at these events end up replicating a similar prototype. See Table 5.1.

While this prototype does not evenly apply to every professional Mexican American's experience, it is common enough that it can be observed consistently in Latinx advocacy spaces. However, the centering of the Mexican American experience in Latinx spaces does limit the narratives of other Latinx groups.

Centering the Mexican American experience in Latinx politics also has the effect of centering Mexican national racial ideology in the racialization of Latinxs. *Mestizaje* in Mexico is a key foundation of national identity. It is a political project, developed in the 20th century by Mexican intellectuals like José Vasconcelos, where members of the nation are homogenized into Mestizos. Mestizos are neither European nor indigenous in Mexican national ideology. As a result, leaders in Mexico have historically claimed that there is no race problem in Mexico since everyone is the same race.

There have been recent movements in the United States to counter the hegemony of Mexican racial ideology and U.S. American racial ideology. U.S. Latinxs have especially begun to tell the stories of Afro-Latinxs, those who are part of the African diaspora whose ancestors were taken to Latin America. Afro-Latinxs are especially prominent in non-Mexican Latin American populations. Many popular musical forms from Latin America are fusions of African and European musical styles (Flores, 2000). African American culture,

Table 5.1 Prototypical narratives of Mexican American success

Prototype	The immigrant narrative	The first-generation narrative
Education	Less formal education. For example, "My parents came here with a fifth-grade education"	Highly educated. For example, "I was able to attend Stanford on scholarship"
Work	Low-skill or entrepreneurial	Professional and/or managerial
Language	Monolingual	Bilingual, English dominant
Values	Hard work, family oriented	Meritocracy, service

especially in the northeastern and southern United States, is an important influence on Latinxs living there. These issues did not arise much in my observation of national conferences. While I do not believe the absence Afro-Latinxs to be intentional, it does have the effect of highlighting some narratives (such as the Mexican American prototype) and deemphasizing others.

It matters who is chosen to represent Latinxs in the United States, and if a whitened, cosmopolitan vision of *Latinidad* is held up, there will be tensions. In *Racism without Racists*, Bonilla-Silva (2010) dedicates a concluding chapter to the "future racial stratification of the United States." He argues that the increased prominence of Latinxs "has already created a number of visible fractures in the United States that seem to be shifting the racial terrain" (177). Specifically, the emergence of Latinxs has disrupted the traditional way of thinking about race in the United States (the binary mode of black versus white) and will prompt the formation of a triracial hierarchal system similar to those found in Latin America and the Caribbean.

According to Bonilla-Silva, the triracial order will comprise whites at the top, "honorary whites" below them, and the "collective black" at the bottom (179). He speculates that the white group will include traditional whites, new white immigrants, "totally assimilated white Latinxs," and light-skinned multiracial people. Honorary whites will include most light-skinned groups of Latinxs and Asian Americans, while the collective black will include African Americans along with dark-skinned Latinxs and Asian Americans. Bonilla-Silva argues that there are several foreseeable problems in this system beyond continuing to place whites at the top of the racial (and thus social and political) hierarchy. First, as in Latin American–styled triracial orders, the large middle buffers discontent between the lowest and highest racial classes. This is similar to how many U.S. Americans, regardless of actual income or wealth, claim to be middle class because of the positive values associated with middle-class identification. Second, this system can actually allow those in power to make claims that "we are all the same" due to the complexity of the racial system and brush aside criticisms of inequity. Bonilla-Silva predicts that this new racial system will ultimately serve as a "formidable fortress for white supremacy" where racial inequality remains while the space to fight it is restricted (179).

Thus, this is the central problem and paradox with pan-ethnic Latinx racial formation driven by elite Latinxs: it purports to represent an entire group of diverse and different people while ultimately only benefiting a professional, socially mobile elite at the top. Many of the main issues raised in this section—the centering of the Mexican American narrative and subtle influence of Mexican national racial ideology, along with the deemphasizing of Afro-Latinxs and other groups—racialize Latinxs in a way that benefits the Latinx elite. The other processes related to homogenization and denationalization highlighted in this chapter synthesize a powerful subject approximating the "new Latinx," who is socially mobile, acculturated, and an ideal consumer.

Networked Latinx identity formation

In this chapter, I have explored the human side of Latinx advocacy in the digital age. Following a multiyear study of national conferences and in-depth interviews with stakeholders, I have outlined the elements and themes unique to the current moment. In summary, several themes stand out. First, the class background of the people who do professional Latinx politics matters. The people who do this work differ dramatically from their constituents in education and professional experience. These backgrounds are hugely influential in their work. Their fluency in elite networks is a resource they draw upon to build alliances among other organizations and to solicit funding. Stakeholders in Latinx advocacy use their social networks as heuristics to make judgments of their audiences. Difference is minimized in this arrangement not by hegemonic media representation but instead by a small class of people producing communication campaigns reflective of their selective networks.

Second, the national identity of Latinxs is deemphasized in favor of U.S. American identity. This happens especially in official fora. Latinx organizations have a long history of emphasizing the Americanness of Latinxs as a means to argue for civil rights. At official fora, this takes the form of a close embrace of the symbology and nationalism of the USA. Dreamers are also held up as prototypical immigrants, worthy of full citizenship by virtue of their achievements. Finally, the narrative of achieving the American Dream is accomplished through a close partnership with large corporations. Latinx representatives of companies like Wal-Mart and Target, brought in through diversity initiatives, share their stories of working their way up and achieving prosperity. These companies are also major sponsors of Latinx groups, so their sponsorship is mutually reinforcing.

However, Latinxs are racialized through the discourse of Latinx advocacy organizations in similar ways to hegemonic media production. Latinxs are racialized as separate and distinct from white and black Americans in the United States, generally refraining from questioning or troubling the racial system of the nation. Recent movements to recognize racial difference among Latinxs or the problematic influences of Mexican racial hegemony were not present in my observations, although if this research were replicated in the future, I expect that it would be on the agenda in some fashion.

References

Bledstein, B. J. (1976). *The culture of professionalism: The middle class and the development of higher education in America.* New York, NY: W.W. Norton.

Bonilla-Silva, E. (2010). *Racism without racists: Color-blind racism and the persistence of racial inequality in the United States.* Lanham, MD: Rowman & Littlefield.

Chuang, A., & Roemer, R. C. (2014). Beyond the positive–negative paradigm of Latino/Latina news-media representations: DREAM Act exemplars, stereotypical selection, and American otherness. *Journalism: Theory, Practice & Criticism, 16*(8), 1045–1061. doi:10.1177/1464884914550974

Dávila, A. M. (2012). *Latinos, Inc: The marketing and making of a people.* Berkeley, CA: University of California Press.

Flores, J. (2000). *From bomba to hip-hop: Puerto Rican culture and Latino identity.* New York, NY: Columbia University Press.

Keith, M. (2005). *After the cosmopolitan?: Multicultural cities and the future of racism.* London, UK: Routledge.

Krogstad, J. (2016, July 28). 5 facts about Latinos and education. Retrieved November 05, 2018, from http://www.pewresearch.org/fact-tank/2016/07/28/5-facts-about-latinos-and-education/

Perez, S. L., & Murray, J. (2016). Latino faces, corporate ties: Latino advocacy organizations and their board membership. *Sociological Forum, 31*(1), 117–137. doi:10.1111/socf.12236

Smith, S. (2017, October 31). Most say American dream is within reach for them. Retrieved November 05, 2018, from http://www.pewresearch.org/fact-tank/2017/10/31/most-think-the-american-dream-is-within-reach-for-them/

6 Latinx presentation, digital representation

The inauguration of Donald Trump as the 44th president of the United States brought large crowds to D.C. on January 20, 2017. Most were there to protest his election at the historic Women's March the day after the official inauguration. The idea for a protest at the inauguration started with the creation of a Facebook event. Thousands of women signed up indicating their interest in marching in Washington, D.C., to protest the president. It is estimated that about 1% of the U.S. population, approximately four million people, participated in the protest. This made the Women's March one of the largest protests ever in U.S. history.

The Women's March inspired other groups to consider taking collective action. Immigrants and activists, many of them Latinx, began to discuss organizing an economic protest after the Women's March in response to calls by Trump to build a wall on the border with Mexico and other anti-immigrant policies. The activists eventually decided to hold their protest on February 16, 2017. The general strike called for immigrants and supporters not to go to work, spend money, or send their children to school for the day. Economic protests, where activists conduct some type of collective action by withholding business, boycotting, or striking, have become increasingly popular in the digital age. As the political system has become ossified to the point where little positive change at the federal level seems possible, economic protests have become much more effective. Using the media and advertisers as vehicles to protest cultural representation or problematic rhetoric has been even more viable, as it has taken down, or greatly diminished the profiles of, conservative media figures like Bill O'Reilly, Rush Limbaugh, and Ann Coulter.

The news of the Day Without Immigrants spread though communication channels typically associated with protest organizing, Facebook and WhatsApp (Robbins, Correal 2017). WhatsApp is especially popular among immigrants in the United States since it allows for international text-based conversations. Initially, no official organization was behind the movement; the protest developed organically. Later, as the protest gained momentum, the Latinx organizations got on board. Using the hashtag #ADayWithoutImmigrants, groups announced their support for the protest and spread the news.

The protest later garnered the support of chefs like Rick Bayless and José Andrés, both of whom announced that they would close their restaurants in solidarity. As Anthony Bourdain once said, most food in the United States is really Mexican or Central American. Immigrants from those countries work in the back of the house in restaurants serving all types of cuisine. Thousands of immigrants participated on the day of the protest, especially in New York City, where the idea for the protest originated. Restaurant workers didn't show up for work. Students stayed home from school. Many faced consequences, too, including hundreds of workers who were fired for missing work. Five teachers and a guidance coordinator at a high school in California cruelly posted on social media that "the average GPA of their classes went up" without the immigrant students there (Phillips, 2017).

The protest was centered in major cities on the coasts. In El Paso, for example, the effects were minimal and it did not disrupt daily life. The protest exemplifies the intersection of collective action with communication technologies in the digital age. In the case of the Day Without Immigrants, digital communication afforded the protesters the ability to spread their message and mobilize new supporters. It also allowed for traditional organizations to get involved at a later stage. In this chapter, I consider the ways in which issues around digital media impact the identity formation and mobilization of U.S. Latinxs.

Choices around what platforms to use and what kinds of messages to send shape what kind of political action is possible. In the case of Latinx identity making, I argue in this chapter that while the results from the past decade of political mobilization are mixed, the construction of a Latinx political identity in the United States has succeeded quite well. Digital platforms and new media did not obliterate the politics of old, as scholars from a decade ago claimed they would. They did, however, present a useful set of tools for powerful interests to create new political and consumer markets and a branded Latinx political identity.

In this chapter, I discuss the results of a series of online case studies surrounding key moments for Latinxs in the United States since the inauguration of Donald Trump as president. I found that the online products created by these organizations reflect the hegemonic structures identified in the previous chapter. Specifically, profession-alized actors created digital content which appeals to professionalized audiences. As I will show, this content also builds upon the themes of Latinx identity formation as well.

In this chapter specifically, I set out to answer the following research question: *How are digital platforms used as sites for mobilizing Latinx voters, and how is identity reified and/or challenged through them?* In the preceding chapter, I discussed the human aspect of Latinx organizing—who the people are who conduct this work and where they come from. In this section, I consider the digital products made by the organizations and the strategies of online communication.

Within this research question, there are two key sub-questions that will structure the results in this chapter. First, *how do stakeholders make strategic choices regarding which media platforms to use and which messages to deliver?* Here, I focus on the politics of platforms and how messages differ between social media and more traditional forms of communication. It is often the case that different organizations use different platforms, usually in recognition of their audiences and their unique characteristics but also due to the skills of the practitioners. The second related sub-question is as follows: *How do organizations respond to developments in the public sphere via communication tools?* In this question, I look more closely at specific events that occurred throughout 2017 and 2018 that directly impacted U.S. Latinxs. The organizations studied in this book were usually reacting to policy announcements, such as the end of DACA; legislative failures, such as the government shutdown over immigration; and primary elections. I use the media created in response to these specific news events related to Latinxs in the United States to do my analysis.

I approach answering each question through the framework laid out in Chapter 2 just as I did in Chapter 4. Instead of using the themes as subheadings, I discuss platform use generally then proceed chrono-logically, moving from the announcement of the end of DACA to the shutdown to the elections in Texas. In each section, I still focus on the themes laid out in Chapter 2. I look at how media created in response to end of DACA or the shutdown relate to the concept of *denationali-zation* or *racialization*. I do this for a practical reason—so readers can more easily follow my argument instead of struggling to piece together news events. I consciously foreground the relationship between organ-izational resources and the kind of communications produced. I do this to center the theoretical tensions I outlined in Chapters 2 and 3 in conversation with the issues around digital organizing I discussed in Chapter 4. As a reminder, the data presented in this chapter is drawn from a qualitative content analysis of organizational communications made around three major news events made in 2018. For a more detailed discussion of the methodology, refer to Chapter 1.

Platforms and messages

As McLuhan said, the medium is the message. Looking at how something is communicated is just as important as analyzing the content of a communication. Among the different media I studied—emails, press releases, and Twitter—the content of messages varied along with the modes of audience interactions. A total of 98 texts were collected, of which 76 were emails. I then separated each set of communications based on the time period. So, in the case of the Texas primary election on March 6, 2018, there were a total of 21 related tweets from the organizations in the sample. Voto Latino (@votoLatinx) tweeted 14 times, and NALEO (@NALEO) tweeted seven times. The other organizations did not have any tweets related to the election. Organizations, of course, sent other tweets, but they were unrelated to the election. See Table 6.1 for more details.

Importantly, the history and human resources of an organization also directly shaped the types of media used to communicate. This insight into organizational communication choices shows why some groups can break into and influence national discussions, while others struggle to get their message out. Hestres (2015) has discussed the differences between "digital first" and "legacy" organizations in their approaches to advocacy. Legacy groups came to use digital communication strategy through adaptation—meaning once the tools became widespread. LULAC is a perfect example of a legacy group embracing digital tools later in the organizational history. Hestres contrasts legacy groups with digital first groups, whose organization identities are directly intertwined with new media.

Table 6.1 Tweets collected by time period

	@ votoLatinx	@ NALEO	@ WeAreUnidosUS	@ LULAC	@ HispanicCaucu
End of DACA	6	6	7	1	11
Shutdown	14	1	2	0	34
Texas primary	21	7	0	0	0

The first dimension to consider is the differences that emerge between communications primarily occurring on social media and those occurring via email and press releases. In the communications I studied, email and press releases were generally used to send one-directional messages. They were not designed to elicit engagement or responses. These messages were meant to report information to members and usually took the form of a statement by organizational leadership. For example, an email from LULAC on January 19, 2018, reissued a press release saying, "Today the United States federal government entered a shutdown with Congress unable to reach a spending bill agreement in time for the midnight deadline. In response, Roger C. Rocha Jr., LULAC National President, issued the following statement …" In general, the communications strategies of LULAC, NALEO, and CHC tended to rely on reporting information through one-directional messages.

The opposite strategy was for organizations to utilize communications that elicited engagement from their audiences. In most cases, this meant social media, but in some examples emails were also written to elicit engagement from the audience. For example, an email from Voto Latino sent on January 20, 2018, said, "We stand with Dreamers and will continue to fight for a permanent DACA solution. So, I'm asking you personally—will you sign our petition to demand that Congress pass the Dream Act?" Clicking on the link took the supporter to a page where they could sign the petition and contribute to Voto Latino. This benefitted Voto Latino by collecting more user-submitted data. These emails followed the model of emails written to encourage donations for political campaigns. Social media from Voto Latino and other organizations (to an extent) also drove users to engage with the information. A common call to action was "retweet to show support for the DREAMers." Organizations that generally used more engaging forms of communication were Voto Latino and UnidosUS.

Organizations that prioritize engagement also have experimented with using elements of Internet culture. GIFs are a popular and humorous form of visual communication. GIFs are widely used on the Internet and are closely related to the concept of memes. Internet memes are jokes, phrases, and pictures that spread quickly whose meaning is created by online sub-cultures. Their popularity rises and falls quickly. A few social media postings collected used memes and GIFs to emphasize textual communication. For example, a tweet from @votolatino on March 6th during the Texas midterm primaries used a dancing GIF from the film *Sisters* (2016) starring Amy Poehler and Tina Fey to congratulate two Latina candidates who won their elections.

For the second dimension of analyzing platform communication, we can directly tie the modes of communication to the institutional histories of the organizations that produce them. The resources available for each group matter as well. In general, organizations with older or professionalized audiences tend to utilize more one-directional forms of communication. LULAC, for example, is the oldest Latinx civil rights organization in the country. It also has the oldest constituency base. The CHC and NALEO both have professionalized constituencies as well. It makes sense for all three organizations that their communications would be more oriented around reporting information to members rather than eliciting engagement. Since these organizations have membership models, annual fees form a major part of funding.

Organizations that use communication oriented around soliciting engagement have audiences that are better understood as followers rather than as members. They approach their audience as a public. These organizations are either newer, like Voto Latino, or resource rich, like UnidosUS. For example, Voto Latino calls itself a civic media organization rather than a civil rights or advocacy group. UnidosUS, which has a longer history and was previously known as the National Council of La Raza, is resource rich. Resources don't just mean funds; they also include human resources, such as staff members with experience in digital media. These organizations have different funding models—relying more on sponsorships rather than membership dues. Engagement-driven media makes sense in this scenario. The audiences and engagement need to be expanded continually to spread the message.

When I first set out to study this topic, I planned to study voter mobilization on platforms like informational websites and mobile applications. Applications like VoterPal were pushed heavily by Latinx civic groups in the lead-up to the 2016 presidential election. VoterPal worked by scanning a non-registered person's ID. It would then use the scanned information to submit a voter registration application to the appropriate jurisdiction. Of course, this method wasn't foolproof; voter registration laws vary tremendously from state to state. The state of Oregon automatically registers voters if they interact with the state in any way—obtaining a driver's license counts. Texas, however, doesn't let voters register online. So in Texas, VoterPal can only email a pre-populated form to the potential voter and then ask them to mail it in to their county elections office.

Despite the drawbacks of VoterPal and other mobile applications or web-based platforms of communication, their absence from all of the forms of communication I studied is worth mentioning. The applications also were not mentioned in interviews. They have been raised in presentations at conventions, which suggests to me that they may have been prioritized in 2017 but deemphasized in 2018. Even around the primary election, this was interesting. Applications I downloaded from each organization, which included the NALEO app, *Opportunidad* (from LULAC), VoterPal (from Voto Latino), and Latinos Vote (from NCLR at the time), had been sparsely updated. In 2018, the homepage of Latinos Vote has only an option to register to vote. It also still displays the name NCLR, which has since been replaced with UnidosUS. The *Opportunidad* app was sparsely updated as well. Besides an option to register to vote, it has sections on immigration and economic empowerment. These sections focus more on the individual than on policy. For example, the immigration section focuses on knowing your rights if stopped by ICE. The economic empowerment section focuses on personal finances rather than any kind of policy reform.

I ultimately decided not to include these applications in my broader research plan because of the lack of content on them. Stromer-Galley (2014) writes in her book, *Presidential Campaigning in the Internet Age*, that political campaigns adjusted to the Internet age by creating platforms that simulated engagement but didn't meaningfully enable true engagement. She calls political websites examples of "controlled interactivity." Voter interaction is reduced to a strategy in her view. In the specific case of these applications, there is a benign neglect of them. They exist but organizational resources are not (or cannot) be devoted to maintaining them. This exemplifies the resource tensions faced by Latinx organizations.

A similar pattern is occurring on these apps, except the result which portends much worse. Since campaigns and civic groups have different aims, it is unwise to utilize applications in a similar way. The problem is based on conceptualizing engagement in a commercial sense (clicks, retweets, sign-ups, etc.) versus conceptualizing engagement in a civic sense (debate, direct action, etc.). This engagement frame is a result of the influence of funding structures. When I worked in a nonprofit's communication department, our foundation reports had to include quantifiable forms of engagement. We used internal social media, website, and email data to show the reach of our work. Discourse change or even civic engagement is harder to quantify for funders. This is further reinforced by how social media platforms like Twitter present engagement as a commercial platform that is used by other commercial entities. For example, it makes a lot of sense for a company to look at their social media engagement through the lens of click-throughs to their website.

In the design phase of this project, I expected to find quite a bit of technological sophistication in the work of Latinx advocacy organizations.

A few months prior to the 2016 election, there was a special forum presented by Google, Univision, and NCLR in Washington, D.C. At the forum, which was held at the Google offices in D.C., officials from each organization excitedly presented a new approach to mobilizing Latinx voters. If a person used the search function on Google to ask something like, "Where can I vote?" or "How can I vote?" they would be directed to a special form where they could check their registration status and polling place. NCLR was keen to note that the form would work in Spanish as it did in English. The officials from NCLR hoped that technology like this could encourage more Latinxs to vote than before.

Embedded in the use of digital technology for civic engagement was the hope among many advocacy groups that increasing access to technology would increase civic participation. This optimistic take was especially prevalent in official discourse before the 2016 election. Lately, it has been much less prevalent. Kreiss (2016) noted that many of the staffers associated with building the digital operations of political campaigns had experience in the high tech industry before entering politics. News reports showed that Facebook offered its expertise to both major 2016 campaigns; the Clinton campaign declined, and Trump accepted their offer. I expected a similar trend of optimism in my own observations but ended up noticing an ambivalence toward digital organizing. All interviewees were drawn from the world of political campaigning and other advocacy work. Their skill sets were focused on organizing and mobilization. While they had experience using software like the Voter Activation Network (VAN) and social media, their technical sophistication was usually limited to those areas. Second, the limited resources of Latinx advocacy organizations impacted the use of digital tech. One subject said that he would love to be able to comb through data and target messages to specific groups, but there was just not enough time in the day. Since his job as a communication director really involved the work of several people (social media director, press secretary, and communication strategist), the bandwidth to do sophisticated digital work was limited. Staffers instead ended up using their social networks online as a heuristic to identify salient political issues and the moods of their constituents. Finally, at the conferences I observed over the summer of 2017, there was a noticeable shift in disposition toward digital tools for organizing. The specter of fake news and disinformation tactics online from the election hung in the air. Panels focused more on protecting oneself online from harassment or data violations. The techno-optimism from the early 2010s had faded and been replaced by technological ambivalence.

The historical trend of a professionalized, even corporatized, form of Latinx civic engagement is reinforced by funder expectations as made clear by Perez and Murray (2016). Platforms of communication clearly matter. Choices about how to communicate with an audience are often reflective of institutional priorities and resources. In the case of Latinx advocacy groups, these choices reveal both the legacy of groups and their disposition toward conceptualizing their audience. The differences in platform and message choice become clear once I discuss the larger themes I've outlined in previous chapters. Over the next few sections, I discuss how platforms are sites of constructing Latinx identity.

The end of DACA

Seemingly drawing inspiration from his reality show experience, Donald Trump announced in August of 2017 that he would come to a decision on the status of DACA. Trump previously had indicated that he might be open to preserving the program, saying that he had a big heart for Dreamers. He was also facing pressure from several Republican Attorney Generals who threatened to sue over the matter. On September 5, 2017, Trump announced that he would end DACA and seek a legislative fix. The reaction by Latinx organizations was swift and overwhelmingly negative.

The organizations appeared to pursue two strategic goals in their response to the DACA announcement. First, they highlighted the profiles of Dreamers to influence public opinion in favor of the program. Second, they pressured members of Congress to find a legislative fix for the immigration issue. The communications from this period resonate with the theoretical framework introduced in Chapter 2. The highlighting of personal accomplishments of DACA recipients evokes the discursive casting of Dreamers as worthy immigrants due to their contributions to the economy and education. Many of the communications produced in this time period reiterate this theme. For example, in a tweet on September 4, Voto Latino (@votolatino) noted that a DACA recipient died in the process of rescuing people affected by Hurricane Harvey in Texas. The framing of DACA recipients as worthy immigrants, essentially emphasizing their Americanness, is a trope of the denationalization of U.S. Latinxs. An email communication from LULAC on August 29, 2017, summed up the rhetorical strategy of framing DACA recipients neatly: "These individuals have served in the military, pursued advanced degrees, and have contributed to the economy."

The strategy to highlight DACA recipients also introduced another element into the Americanizing of U.S. Latinxs: the potential economic impact of rescinding DACA. UnidosUS (@WeAreUnidos) tweeted an image on September 2017 stating "DACA works. Period." and that "Beneficiaries would contribute an estimated $460 BILLION to the U.S. economy over the next ten years." In the image, they advocate on the behalf of DACA recipients using their potential economic productivity as an argument for their legalization as citizens. The rhetorical framing here is part of the collapsing of the distinction between political subject and economic subject. This is a prime example of the mode of thinking associated with neoliberalism. Immigrant rights are justified on the basis of their economic productivity. This language is another example of the denationalization of Latinxs in the United States and the renationalizing of them as economic subjects in U.S. capitalism. Latinxs in this frame are worthy of inclusion in the U.S. body politic only if they are contributing members of society. In this case, contributing really means productive and society means the economy. Well-meaning immigrant rights activists help contribute to this framing when they say undocumented immigrants pay taxes and work hard.

Dame-Griff (2016) has discussed how the literal bodies of Latinx people, often marked as overweight or obese, prevent their full acceptance as citizens and mark them as foreign (165–167). In a speech to an NLCR convention, First Lady Michelle Obama rhetorically connected the bad mothering of Latinas to an "epidemic of childhood obesity" among brown bodies. Latina moms (and other maternal figures) were loving their children to death by feeding them "unhealthy" ethnic comfort foods. Obama's speech is an iteration of her *Let's Move!* Campaign, which focused on reducing childhood obesity. The rhetoric of the worthy immigrant is on plain view here and in the tweets of these national organizations.

In their response to the end of DACA, advocacy organizations developed a political strategy that employed the rhetoric and framing I've discussed before: attempting to influence members of Congress to pass legislation to fix DACA. In their rhetoric, they often implied that voting to support DACA would be electorally beneficial to those who did so. They intimated that Latinx voters would reward politicians who looked out for them. However, advocacy groups indicated that they would also remember who voted against them and punish them electorally. This rhetoric evokes the electoral mythology of the sleeping giant narrative. Beltran (2010) writes that the notion of the Latinx electorate as a sleeping giant, waiting to awaken in response to anti-Latinx or pro-Latinx politics, is a common feature of advocacy rhetoric. According to Beltran, the sleeping giant is a metaphor that simultaneously presents Latinxs as a potentially powerful voting bloc as well as a passive group. They are passive because they are dependent upon the political strategy and rhetoric of others to be mobilized. The metaphor of the sleeping giant shows elements of the minimization of difference and the racialization of Latinxs. Homogeny of political values is assumed in the construction of sleepy Latinx voters waiting to be mobilized by a specific political message.

Racialization is done via the sleeping giant metaphor in a unique way. There has been a tendency by Latinx political professionals to conceptualize the constituency of Latinx voters in similar ways to other ethnic constituencies, especially African Americans. Here, the racialization of Latinxs works by conceptualizing them as a group who can be mobilized by specific issues of identity politics, similar to how African Americans can be mobilized as a community by salient issues. For political professionals, especially those with experience in national presidential campaigns, this constituency heuristic is a widely accepted one.

Organizations utilized this rhetoric in their messages about and toward members of Congress. For example, Voto Latino (@votolatino) praised Republican Senator Lindsey Graham for his state's support for DACA. The implicit message to other Republicans was to get on board with protecting DACA or face consequences. In 2012, following the loss of Mitt Romney to Barack Obama, the GOP produced an autopsy analyzing their loss (Edsall, 2013). They concluded that their general dismissal of minority voters, especially Latinxs, could be the end of the party electorally. They also said that their only other pathway to political power besides inclusivity would be to mobilize an increasing percentage of the shrinking white vote. Recent history has shown a move further in the latter direction, but the autopsy shows that the idea of moderating on immigration to appeal to more Latinxs originated with the Republican National Committee.

The end of DACA showcases many of the ideological fissures in contemporary politics and the uncertainty of where U.S. Latinxs fit in as a constituency. Latinx political leadership in this moment attempted to do their best to combat the reactionary politics of the Trump administration by highlighting the contributions of Dreamers and by pressuring members of Congress with the implicit threat that Latinx voters would remember the policies they supported. Both strategies resonate with the ideological themes of Latinx identity formation, such as denationalization and homogenization.

The shutdown

The announced end of DACA set up an inevitable confrontation in Congress over the issue. It came to a head in the days leading up to January 20, 2018, when appropriate funding to keep the government open would expire. In recent years, using the end of funding and the threat of a government shutdown has become a feature of U.S. politics. This is probably due to the otherwise general inability of Congress to pass anything meaningful under normal procedures without one party in a supermajority. Democrats, who in 2018 were in the minority in both the House and the Senate, hoped to use the shutdown to extract policy concessions from Republicans on immigration. The shutdown of the government officially happened on January 20 after Democrats in the Senate filibustered a temporary extension of funding. The shutdown ended after the weekend. Democrats voted to fund the government after a promise by Republican leadership to hold debate on DACA legislation before it expired.

Most of the communications produced in the period of the shutdown implored members of Congress to "stand with" Dreamers. The shutdown was also portrayed to be the fault of Republicans. No criticism of the Democratic Party came from official communications. Both themes share a similarity in how they are framed. Organizational rhetoric around DACA is usually framed to members of Congress as "being on the right side of history." This frame is a relatively new one in political rhetoric. Looking backward from current times, political moments like the passage of the Civil Rights Act are framed as courageous votes by lawmakers. A similar rhetorical frame was associated with the issue of same sex marriage. Immigration reform has thus been canonized into a long history of struggle alongside the civil rights and LGBTQ rights movements. Recent political history is, in turn, framed reflexively, meaning that the message to lawmakers is to vote with their minds on how future generations will view them. These groups deploy the fear of historical judgment as a communication strategy. They intimate that eventually their side will win out (as history is on their side) and they will write the story in the future.

This frame resonates with the notion of "standing with" Dreamers. The frame of standing up is a constant feature in the communications around DACA. It is usually used in messaging directed toward members of Congress imploring them to take a specific action. For example, an email from Voto Latino sent on January 17, 2018, asked recipients to "not let him [Trump] keep getting away with his racist attacks. Sign your name to condemn Trump's racism and stand up for immigrants!" The link then took recipients to a page where they could sign up for more information from Voto Latino and even donate to the organization. LULAC used similar language in a press release signed by Roger Rocha, the national president at the time. In it, he said, "LULAC continues to stand with DACA recipients and urge Congress to pass the Dream Act now." The active language of standing with someone (in this case, a constituency) is a call to action. The implicit message is that for those who sit out, there will be electoral consequences.

Members of Congress were not targeted equally. Public pressure was directed toward Republicans. Democrats were directly challenged in very few communications. After the shutdown, there was no criticism of Democrats in Congress in organizational communications. This is due to the fact that many of these organizations, while being officially non-partisan, are closely connected to the institutional Democratic Party. For example, in June of 2018, former Housing and Urban Development Secretary Julián Castro—a Democrat who was then considered by some to be a potential 2020 candidate for president and later did run—joined the board of Voto Latino. Many of their communications reiterate Democratic positions on issues. It is unclear if they are following the messaging lead from Democrats or vice versa. As we will see, the close association with the Democratic Party extends to involvement in electoral politics.

Closeness to the Democratic Party so far has not resulted in what Kreiss (2016) observed in his book on the technological developments of the Democratic and Republican parties. He found that over the past few years, a network of technologically minded staffers emerged out of innovative campaigns and party initiatives. Technical staffers came to campaigns from the tech industry, then went on to found their own firms, which then contracted with the party. In short, new networks of actors were created. While campaign talent from the Clinton campaign went on to work for Latinx groups, they primarily had field organizing and communications experience rather than technical experience. Thus, the Clinton campaign talent was entirely willing and able to import the ideological frames and communication approaches of the establishment Democratic Party. Yet, the technological expertise—building data collection and analysis systems—was not as present.

Titles in an organization are important here, as they signal what kind of expectations and resources are allocated to a department. Kreiss notes, for example, that early campaigns used to relegate the data office as a subsidiary of communications. The communications team ended up being more focused on traditional media. As digital campaigning matured, data moved into its own separate office in the organizational chart. It then began to influence the strategy and tactics of every part of the campaign. Data would influence fundraising strategies and messaging. The organizations I profiled in my study often collapsed the two, data and communications, into a communications role. Thus, this partly accounts for the lack of more sophisticated data operations. Because the distinction has been collapsed, it seems a more traditional sense of doing communications work has surfaced—dealing with the press, crafting messages, etc.—rather than the more cutting-edge practices.

The 2018 Texas Democratic primary

On March 6, 2018, Democratic voters in the state of Texas selected the Democrats who would represent their party in the November general election. Texas has been a Republican stronghold for years; no Democrat has held statewide office since the 1990s. Among political practitioners in the state, there has been a dream of turning Texas blue by activating its Latinx voting population. Compared to states like California and Nevada, Latinxs in Texas are registered and vote at much lower rates. Partly, this is due to the lack of civic infrastructure, as one interview subject explained to me. Private sector unions are basically nonexistent in the state. In Nevada, unions can mobilize thousands of Latinx voters for elections easily. Barreto and Segura (2014) write that Latinxs in California were mobilized by the anti-immigrant governorship of Pete Wilson and have been reliable Democratic voters since the 1990s.

The notion that Latinxs in Texas would be reliable Democratic voters is much less certain. In the 2014 gubernatorial election, 30% of Latinxs—mostly men—voted for Republican Greg Abbott. Left-leaning organizations still have had their eye on the prize of turning Texas blue. An organization of former Obama campaign alums called Battleground Texas was formed after 2012 to register and mobilize voters. The 2018 primaries were the first federal elections to be held in the Trump era in Texas. They were also among the first major primaries of 2018 nationwide. The Latinx groups I studied were involved at various levels in the primary. Some commented from afar; others mobilized on the ground level. The rhetoric they utilized around elections is interesting and resonates with many of the themes of this book.

After reviewing countless pieces of communication, I was surprised to encounter few messages in Spanish. Finally, the first instance of Spanish language appeared in a communication produced by NALEO (@NALEO). The message was simple, relaying the times that early voting sites would be open in Texas and encouraging voters to vote early. One tweet said, *"La communidad Latina es el futuro de Texas."* The relative lack of Spanish in other communications is striking. It only appears sometimes in the form of well-known words, such as *adelante* or *basta*, in English-language posts. Indeed, all of the conferences I attended in the summer conducted all of their official business in English. If Spanish was spoken, it was done in unofficial spaces. This is a relic of the era of legitimacy in Latinx politics, a social and political moment when conditions forced Latinxs in the United States to adopt the use of English to fit in. This is also a clear example of the denationalizing trend in Latinx politics.

Spanish-language messages can be effective in mobilizing Latinxs. A study by Panagopoulos and Green (2010) found that Spanish-language radio advertisements were effective in increasing turn-out during the get-out-the-vote (GOTV) phase of an election, which typically occurs toward the end when likely voters are reminded to vote. GOTV is not a time to convince new voters to vote for your campaign. Other instances show the effectiveness of Spanish in mobilizing Latinxs. Spanish-language ballots in California increased the turnout of Spanish-only voters (Hopkins, 2011), and phone calls from real people speaking Spanish increased Latinx turnout in a NALEO campaign from 2005 (Ramírez, 2005).

The rhetorical framing of history also reemerged in the communications around the Texas primary. Voters were asked to "make history" by electing the first Latina congressional members from Texas. Republicans in Congress dealing with the DACA issue were asked to be on the right side of history, framing history as a force outside of any one person's control. History, in that case, is a force, something that acts upon people. In the case of Texas voters, voters were framed as having more agency—they could shape and make history with their votes. The subjects in the case of making history were two Latinas running for Congress in Houston and El Paso, respectively, Sylvia Garcia and Veronica Escobar. Both ended up winning their respective primaries in heavily Democratic districts and won their election for Congress in the fall. Beyond mobilizing Latinx voters, organizations also support Latinx politicians. NALEO, for example, represents Latinx elected officials and advances their interests. Voto Latino has a political action committee called the VL Action Network. The VL Action Network supported both Sylvia Garcia and Veronica Escobar in their elections in Texas.

Their rhetoric focused on making history by electing two Latinas from Texas to Congress. This is significant because even though Houston and El Paso have sizeable Latinx populations, they have only recently had non-white representatives in Congress. An email from Voto Latino stated, "There are great candidates on the ballot to represent El Paso, like Veronica Escobar who would be the first Latina to represent Texas in Congress! Find your nearest polling location and head to the polls on March 6th!" These messages were also repeated over several different types of media, including text messages and social media. I personally received a text message from a real person reminding me to vote. As one interview subject stressed to me, Voto Latino was an early innovator in using text messaging to mobilize supporters, and it is now widely used in the industry.

The messaging around the elections in Texas evoked debates around identity politics and specifically the politics of representation. The politics of representation refers to a political goal of electing people representative of groups who have traditionally not been in elected office. A critical element of the argument is that greater diversity of representation will lead to greater social equity for marginal groups. The argument is that "representation matters," and that young people need to see figures like them in positions of power. Psychology literature suggests that positive representations of people with a similar ethnic background are beneficial for adolescents (Hughes, Toro, Way, 2017). Women in corporate leadership positions generally correlate with better business outcomes and less risky decision making (Chen, Crossland, Huang, 2014). It is less clear that the claim that more representation will lead to increased social equity can be proven in any empirical sense. The critique of representational politics is that it favors placing avatars symbols of progress instead of reforming or changing the systems and institutions that led to the gross social inequality in the first place. After the results were in and both Latinas won their elections, messages of congratulations abounded across communication channels. National attention as well as organizational attention moved back to DACA and other issues soon afterward.

New tools, old practices?

While the project of increasing the Latinx electorate has been partially successful over the past decade—there are, of course, many barriers beyond media to increasing Latinx voting—the project of developing a new Latinx identity has been a striking success. Digital tools have been at the forefront of helping to shape this new political identity. I argue that recent political events have helped accelerate it as well. Having analyzed the communications and strategy around three salient events—the announced end of DACA, the government shutdown of 2018, and the 2018 Texas primary election—here are some conclusions.

First is a lesson in research design for the field of communication. Digital content told part of the story about Latinx organizations in 2018, but more data points were needed to facilitate a more in-depth analysis. Unlike political or advertising campaigns, the digital products created by nonprofit organizations just do not scale or scope wide enough to analyze them in isolation. I found myself often referring back to conversations I had at conferences and in my interviews to give greater context to the production of messages and discourses on digital media. Instead of analyzing these messages and discourses as discrete units, scholars should consider digital media as an artifact existing within a system of production. The whole system that produces an artifact needs to be analyzed.

Second, the platform on which something is transmitted matters. Messages vary in their structure depending upon whether they are sent on engagement-driven platforms or not. The choices around what kinds of platforms are used to communicate also very much depend on the institutional history and resources of an organization. Older and less resourced organizations tend to stick to one-directional media, like email or press releases. Newer and resource-richer organizations tend to use more dynamic engagement communication. This is due to the difference in how groups conceptualize their audiences—as members or as a public. On engagement-driven platforms, calls to action have also shifted away from purely digital asks, such as signing a petition or signing up on a website. Trump-era politics have shifted calls to action to on-the-ground activities, like protest and civic participation. In contrast, the one-directional messages still generally focus on informing members about ongoing political issues and what the organization is doing to fight them.

Third, the themes of Latinx socialization are highly present on digital media. The message that Dreamers are American in all but paperwork has continually been reinforced online during the events presented in this chapter. The elections in Texas with the focus on electing Latina candidates also reinforced the homogenization of Latinxs in the United States by tying their backgrounds to a narrative of Latinx social and political advancement. The immigration controversies have also further racialized the politics of immigration and Latinxs. The two concepts—Latinx identity and immigration politics—are becoming intertwined, especially in the age of Trump and the ideology of white reactionary politics.

References

Barreto, M. A., & Segura, G. M. (2014). *Latino America: How America's most dynamic population is poised to transform the politics of the nation.* New York, NY: PublicAffairs.

Beltran, C. (2010). *The trouble with unity: Latino politics and the creation of identity.* Oxford, UK: Oxford University Press.

Chen, G., Crossland, C., & Huang, S. (2014). Female board representation and corporate acquisition intensity. *Strategic Management Journal, 37*(2), 303–313. doi:10.1002/smj.2323

Dame-Griff, E. C. (2016). "He's not heavy, he's an anchor baby": Fat children, failed futures, and the threat of Latina/o excess. *Fat Studies, 5*(2), 156–171. doi:10.1080/21604851.2016.1144233

Edsall, T. (2013, March 20). The Republican autopsy report. Retrieved November 08, 2018, from https://opinionator.blogs.nytimes.com/2013/03/20/the-republican-autopsy-report/

Hestres, L. E. (2015). Climate change advocacy online: Theories of change, target audiences, and online strategy. *Environmental Politics, 24*(2), 193–211. doi:10.1080/09644016.2015.992600

Hopkins, D. J. (2011). Translating into votes: The electoral impacts of Spanish-language ballots. *American Journal of Political Science, 55*(4), 814–830. doi:10.1111/j.1540-5907.2011.00534.x

Hughes, D. L., Toro, J. D., & Way, N. (2017). Interrelations among dimensions of ethnic-racial identity during adolescence. *Developmental Psychology, 53*(11), 2139–2153. doi:10.1037/dev0000401

Kreiss, D. (2016). *Prototype politics: Technology-intense campaigning and the data of democracy.* Oxford, UK: Oxford University Press.

Panagopoulos, C., & Green, D. P. (2010). Spanish-language radio advertisements and Latino voter turnout in the 2006 congressional elections. *Political Research Quarterly, 64*(3), 588–599. doi:10.1177/1065912910367494

Perez, S. L., & Murray, J. (2016). Latino faces, corporate ties: Latino advocacy organizations and their board membership. *Sociological Forum, 31*(1), 117–137. doi:10.1111/socf.12236

Phillips, K. (2017, February 19). These California teachers mocked students for skipping school on immigrant boycott day. Retrieved November 08, 2018, from https://www.washingtonpost.com/news/education/wp/2017/02/19/these-california-teachers-mocked-students-for-skipping-school-on-immigrant-boycott-day/

Ramírez, R. (2005). Giving voice to Latino voters: A field experiment on the effectiveness of a national nonpartisan mobilization effort. *The ANNALS of the American Academy of Political and Social Science, 601*(1), 66–84. doi:10.1177/0002716205278422

Robbins, L., & Correal, A. (2017, February 16). On a 'day without immigrants'. Workers show their presence by staying home. Retrieved November 08, 2018, from https://www.nytimes.com/2017/02/16/nyregion/day-without-immigrants-boycott-trump-policy.html

Stromer-Galley, J. (2014). *Presidential campaigning in the Internet age.* New York, NY: Oxford University Press.

7   Media coverage of the 2018 midterms

The summer of 2018 placed the borderlands, immigrants, and Latinx voters squarely in the public agenda. News about the family separation policy of the Trump administration provoked a fierce opposition to the dehumanizing and cruel developments. Latino organizations swiftly organized in protest. By the end of the summer, the most egregious elements of the migrant crisis were minimized, although the fundamental problems still remained. What followed was instructive on the changing dynamics of how Latinx voters are framed in the media.

A common refrain heard at protests, one of which I observed in Tornillo, Texas, was that Latinxs needed to see this crisis as an inspiration to mobilize for the 2018 midterm elections. They needed to make their voices heard, according to organizers—and the Democrats who hoped to get their votes to regain control in Congress. This proposition that the family separation crisis would lead to energized Latinx voters would also be a staple of media coverage in the weeks leading up to the elections. An NBC News headline read, "Family separations at the border help fuel new Latino voter drive." The article detailed efforts by Voto Latino to mobilize Latinx voters with the hope that the actions and language of the Trump administration would rile voters up (Przybyla, 2018).

Democrats in the 2018 midterm elections won enough seats in the House of Representatives to win control back. A study from the Latino Policy & Politics Initiative at UCLA focused on Latinx voter turnout in eight key states in the 2018 midterm election. Overall, they found that there was substantial growth in ballots cast in majority Latinx precincts. They argued that the vote growth in these precincts was responsible for the flipping of multiple House seats for Democrats (Wilcox-Archuleta, Gutierrez, Baretto, Diaz, Oaxaca, 2018). For example, 59% of precincts where Latinxs were the majority saw an increase of over 70% in ballots cast when compared to the midterm elections of 2014.

The 2018 Senate elections proved more complicated. The close nature of the Texas senate race between incumbent Republican Ted Cruz and Democrat Beto O'Rourke can partially be attributed to the rise of Latinx voters. O'Rourke lost the election with 48.3% of the votes. However, this was the best result statewide for a Democrat in Texas since 1978. The percentage increases among Latinx voters could simply mean that there are more eligible Latinx voters than in 2014—a young population will have more 18-year-old voters every year. It is much harder to claim that the rhetoric of Donald Trump caused an increase in Latinx voters. For example, Arizona voters elected a Democratic Senator (alongside a Republican Governor) and Latinx voters in Florida helped re-elect a Republican Senator and Governor. Varied results led to varied narratives.

The results of the 2018 midterm election are worth analyzing in the context of this book due to the coverage generated after the news event. Specifically, this chapter is concerned with how the results of the election were framed in news coverage following the election. The following sections deal with the immediate news coverage two weeks after the midterm election. A descriptive summary of results is presented first, then followed by sections discussing the themes of racialization, denationalization, and homogenization found in the coverage.

How the media talked about Latinx voters

Starting on election night, the role Latinx voters played in winning the House back for Democrats was a popular discussion point for national newspapers, online news, and cable news. Using a variety of parameters described in the methodology section of Chapter 1, 104 news items were analyzed. A breakdown of the 104 news sources is presented in Table 7.1.

Overall, news sources overwhelmingly racialized Latinx voters as separate and distinct from other voters. Homogenization of Latinx voters was less common, but still prevalent. The denationalization of Latinx voters was almost non-existent. Stories could be coded as all three categories or none at all. These categories can be seen in Table 7.2.

Table 7.1 Data by news medium

News source	Newspaper	Online News	Cable news	Magazine
Total	23 (22.1%)	29 (27.9%)	47 (45.2%)	5 (4.8%)

Table 7.2 Themes of U.S. Latinx identity making in news coverage

Theme	Homogenization	Denationalization	Racialization
Total	43 (41.3%)	6 (5.8%)	93 (89.4%)

Table 7.3 Counter themes of U.S. Latinx identity making in news coverage

Theme	Counter homogenization	Counter denationalization	Counter racialization
Total	25 (24%)	8 (7.7%)	3 (2.9%)

In addition, I also encountered several news articles which displayed frames which countered the themes theorized in Chapter 2. These news articles disputed or challenged homogenizing, denationalizing, and racializing narratives about Latinx voters. Stories could be coded as all three categories or none at all. Instances of each counter narrative were coded separately and presented in Table 7.3.

Minimization of difference

As seen in Table 7.2, the homogenization of Latinx voters was a consistent theme of media coverage following the election. Latinx voters were generally framed in the news as a homogenous bloc of voters waiting to be captured by Democrats and perilously falling out a reach for Republicans. Two consistent frames emerged. First, Latinx voters were described as a rising demographic force in electoral politics. Second, Latinx voting was tied to immigration issues. Few articles countered the homogenization of Latinx voters, but the few are discussed at the end of this section.

The frame of the rising Latinx electorate closely follows what Beltran (2010) called the sleeping giant narrative. If just enough Latinx voters could be awoken to political reality, they would be a determining force in politics. 2002 also saw the publication of the *Emerging Democratic Majority* by political scientists John B. Judis and Ruy Texiera. In it, they argued that demographic changes such as the increase in non-white population would produce a consistent winning coalition for the Democratic Party. The idea of demographic destiny still seems to have the most currency with party leaders and media pundits.

For example, Orange County, CA, a long time bastion of conservatism, in the 2018 midterm elections completely flipped for the

Democrats. The reasons according to the media? Changing demographics. An article from Mother Jones described a newly Democratic district as being known "as predominantly white, wealthy, and conservative, but a growing Latino population and redistricting in 2011 have nudged it to the left" (Schatz, 2018). The increase in Latinx voters was attributed the success of California Democrats along with elections in Nevada and Texas. A National Public Radio report claimed, "Latinos there have played a key role for Democrats" in Nevada (2018).

The categorization of Latinx voters as an increasing cause of Democratic victory homogenizes them as a passive electoral force. It is also not a stretch to image how framing Latinx voters as increasing in numbers and as a population influx leads to far-right racist rhetoric of an invasion of Latinx immigrants. The massacre in El Paso in August 2019 was committed by a white supremacist who believed in the racist replacement theory. The framing of Latinx voters as a homogenous catalyst for transformation in the U.S. American Southwest, including an article titled "Don't Look Now, but the Mountain West Is Turning Blue" in *the Daily Beast* (Mair, 2018), also centers how the western states play a symbolic role in U.S. American culture. The west is a cultural stand in for frontierism and adventurism. In other words, the Wild West still figures prominently in the cultural imagination of Americans as a place where the future takes place and the potential of the nation lies. As Latinx voters are figuratively framed as taking over the west, opportunistic right-wing demagogues will take advantage. Donald Trump in a September 2019 rally in New Mexico went as far as to say, "Who do like more—the country or the Hispanics?" to a prominent Latino supporter and speaking broadly about his relationship with Latinx voters.

Immigration as a major issue relevant to Latinx voters is another key aspect of homogenization found in the mainstream media coverage following the 2018 elections. Several articles attributed the increase in Latinx voters as a reaction toward President Donald Trump's rhetoric about immigrants. It was also a very common refrain from pundits on cable news shows. Notably, the weeks before the election, President Trump focused in on the supposed danger of a migrant caravan heading toward the U.S.-Mexican border. It seems that he hoped this immigration panic spectacle would win over last minute undecided voters. The media framed Senate victories in Arizona and House victories in California as defeats for this strategy. A New York Times article noted:

> Mr. Trump's focus on a hardline immigration policy in the final
> weeks turned off both Latino voters and independents, who make

up Arizona's largest voting bloc. That has not gone unnoticed by Democrats, who will certainly keep a close eye on the Sun Belt as they turn their focus to 2020.

(Steinhauer, Dias 2018)

Other news sources posited similar conclusions that the focus on immigration would make the western states competitive for Democrats in 2020 and beyond.

Of the news items which presented a counter homogenizing frame, essentially arguing that there are differences among Latinx voters, there were generally two kinds of stories. First, some stories and news pundits simply acknowledged that not all Latinx voters are the same. Rachel Maddow, a host on MSNBC, noted that "there is no single Latino community in the United States. There's a lot of different types of Latino communities with a lot of different geographic concerns and different ideological alliances" in response to another panelist on an election night edition of *Hardball with Chris Matthews* (2018). In response, the other panelist added that many Latinx voters, especially in Florida, have historically voted Republican for ideological reasons. The other general framing came from conservative figures in the press, such as the *Wall Street Journal*, whose interest is to frame Latinx voters as not totally homogenous. An article from the journal attributed Senate and Gubernatorial wins in Arizona and Florida to Latinx voter's affinity for school choice and charter schools (2018). In these limited cases, the difference of Latinx voter issue concerns was used to advocate for conservative politics.

Denationalization

The discursive shedding of Latin American national identities and rechristening as U.S. Americans, the process of denationalization in Latinx identity formation, was not as common in mainstream media coverage of the 2018 midterms. Coverage of Latinx issues in the mainstream press is still scarce enough, that even having a body of texts to analyze is a challenge. Denationalization occurs broadly when even Latinx voters are mentioned of course, since to vote they must be citizens, but such a categorization would render the term less useful. Instead, this section will focus on a few key instances of denationalizing and counter-denationalizing frames in the news media.

I argue that the lack of denationalizing frames (connecting Latinx voters to the United States) is part of a larger structuralized view in the mainstream press which still views Latinx people as foreign or as a threat (Chavez, 2013) to the United States. Latinx organizations like the ones profiled earlier in this book consciously engage in de-nationalization themselves to present Latinx people are authentically American in response. Nevertheless, the most common instances of denationalization in press coverage focused on defining Latinx voters in Florida. Often, news stories would casually describe that Florida Latinx voters are historically more conservative and Republican lean-ing than other Latinxs in the Southwest, thus ignoring the historical and ideological differences among Latinx voters in the state. These historical differences also led to different structures of opportunities for the parties in Florida, with the Republican Party actively courting Latinx voters. An article in the *Washington Post*, for example, said:

> Florida remains a top concern heading into the 2020 elections, when the state will probably play a crucial role in any path for Trump to win a second term. Contrary to the Latino vote else-where in the country, the Cuban, Puerto Rican and Central American populations in the Sunshine State split more evenly, as Gov. Rick Scott (R) mounted an aggressive outreach effort.
>
> (Balz, Scherer, 2018)

Denationalizing Florida Latinx voters, who have come to the state from a variety of Latin American countries for reasons as varied as be-ing political refugees, economic migrants, ecological disaster refugees, and internal migrants, renders national differences blurry. Glazing over these differences, which often results in different ideological alli-ances and coalitional identities in Florida politics, paints Latinx voters with the same broad brush and lacks a means to account for why some Latinx voters in Florida just happen to vote for Republicans.

Counter-denationalization was simply more common in media texts following the election. While Latinx organization consciously tries to emphasize their Americanness through the use of American symbol-ogy and the use of the English language, media texts focus on the use of Spanish and foreignness. For example, an article started by stating, "On the morning of Election Day, the top trending search on Google was '*donde votar*,' which means 'where to vote' in Spanish," which positioned that Latinx voters are the primary drivers of this trend (Bowden, 2018). The article went on to note that a county in Idaho of-fered Spanish language ballots for the first time in 2018. Even though turnout rose, it also rose in nearby districts not offering Spanish lan-guage ballots, so the effect on voter turnout was difficult to discern. Another article in USA Today focused on voter suppression in Dodge

City, Kansas. Local officials had moved the sole polling location in the county outside the city limits—where it was difficult to travel without a car. A source from Voto Latino claimed that the issues in Dodge City were similar to voter suppression issues nationwide. The article also cited a 19-year-old Latinx man, who said, 'Honestly, I don't know what the election is all about … nobody has told me anything about anything' (Hughes, 2018). Other articles focused on Latinx voters who are immigrants and as Spanish speakers. The effect of stories like these reinforces the foreignness of Latinx voters. However, given the rareness of such media texts, it indicates that denationalizing Latinx voters is more of strategy used by Latinx organizations to frame and mobilize their constituencies. Organizations denationalize and Americanize their constituencies in response to the discursive framing of Latinxs as foreign and dangerous from politicians like Donald Trump as he famously said in his campaign launch and in the mainstream press.

Racialization

Compared to denationalization, racialization was extremely common. Most news media texts analyzed for this chapter racialized Latinx voters as a separate and distinct group from white and black voters. Racialization as a process ignores the racial difference highly present in Latin America and discursively frames Latinx people as their own unique and different group in the United States. Hand in hand with the separateness is the supposition that Latinx voters have ideological and policy priorities which make them a bounded racial political category. Racialization as a process in media texts took two primary forms. First, Latinx voters were often framed as members of a coalition of voters supporting Democratic candidates. The phrase "Blacks and Latinos" was a common one. Second, the sources which pushed this narrative tended to be overwhelming mainstream news pundits.

The prominence of Latinx voters in electoral contests has challenged a system which has long operated according to a white/black binary (Bonilla-Silva, 2010). The media texts published immediately following the 2018 midterms seem to have resolved this challenge by framing Latinx voters as a similarly corporate and bounded racial group as Black voters. Common frames included phrasing such as "this candidate's win can be attributed to increases in votes from Black and Latino voters" or "the president's rhetoric has turned off Black and Latino voters." An article in the Atlantic, for example, focused on voter suppression efforts by Georgia Secretary of State and Republican candidate for Governor Brian Kemp directed toward "Black and

Latino" voters (Newkirk, 2018a). Another article covering results from Wisconsin results said, "the limited data available on the Wisconsin race suggest that increased turnout among black and Latino voters was one of the biggest shifts from the 2014 midterms to this election" (Newkirk, 2018b). Rhetorically tying together these two racial groups positions them as separate, even though these two identities are closely intertwined in Latin America and in U.S. history.

The framing of Black and Latino voters also positions them as members of the Democratic coalition. Jesse Jackson in his run for the Democratic nomination for President in 1988 called his base the "rainbow coalition." The coalition of voters was multicultural and multiethnic. Barack Obama in his 2008 election would use the rainbow coalition principle in appealing to a wide variety of voters. That election presaged the general sorting in party constituencies. Democrats increasingly became the party of urban and non-white voters, while Republicans became the party of rural and white voters (Abramowitz, 2010). Media texts that racialize Latinx voters also do so by placing them within the winning coalition formula for Democrats—Senator Bernie Sanders in an appearance on Politics Nation on MSNBC days after the midterm repeated this framing, saying, "We have got to bring our coalition together. That means working people who are black and white and Latino, Asian-American, native-American to demand that we have an economy and a government that works for all" (2018).

Racializing Latinx voters as a category of voters similar to Black and other groups of voters shapes their identity as a homogenous racial entity. It transforms diverse Latinxs experiences into an easily consumable narrative—children of immigrants, handworkers, socially conservative, brand loyal—the symbolic markers outlined in Chapter 2. Language slippage is important here too, as it suggests preferred narratives. Changing out Mexican American history for a broader idea of Latinx history is a common sleight of hand. For example, MSNBC host Chris Matthews on Hardball said, "Bobby was the first mainstream American politician to take up the cause of the Latino farmworkers in California, joining in a religious bond with the great Cesar Chavez" discussing coalitional politics (2018). The racialization of Latinx voters also further racializes other groups in the United States. It makes set us differences between Black and Latinx voters as differences of political and policy interest. The tying of immigration to Latinx voters in mainstream discourse can also be used as a wedge with other groups, especially white voters.

It should be noted that racializing rhetoric in the media often comes from pundits and writers who do not seem to be that familiar with

Latinx people themselves. References to Latinx voters as a distinct racial group with its own priorities came from sources in the media who did not have an obvious expertise in Latinx politics. Instead, they have general knowledge about U.S. politics. Theresa Vargas (2018), a Washington Post writer, observed

> Take Latino voters. Every time I hear people express shock that not all of them hate Trump based on his anti-immigrant policies, I want to fling open my laptop and pull up my Facebook page to show them the regular political sparring among relatives and high school classmates of mine with last names such as Acosta, Garcia and Ochoa. I want to remind them that many Latinos have such deep roots in this country that expecting them to empathize with new immigrants is no different from expecting a fourth-generation Irish American to do so.

Other examples of counter racializing rhetoric were rare in the media texts collected.

Telling the Latinx story

The framing of the rise and characteristics of Latinx voters is a part of a larger news media narrative around changing demographics in the United States, partisan realignment, and national politics in the 2010s. Latinx voters are used as background characters (or even as props) in a larger drama around political rituals such as elections, campaigns, and news events. The 2016 and 2018 elections featured Latinx people and voters in prominent places. In 2016, President Donald Trump launched his campaign attacking Mexican immigrants and proposed harsher immigration policies. The news media, along with many Latinx organizations as well, predicted that Trump would encourage more Latinx voters to show up on election day. The results were largely inconclusive. It was harder to make a claim that Latinx voters played a decisive role when Trump won surprisingly. The 2018 election proved to be a more coherent narrative. President Trump deliberately fanned anti-immigrant sentiment in the days before the midterm elections hoping that it would prove just as successful as it did in the previous election. Pundits again predicted that this would lead to increased Latinx turnout and a victory for Democratic candidates for the House and Senate. When the results conformed to this prediction, a ready-made narrative was set.

The connections between Latinx political organizations and the news media are also evident in the media texts studied in this chapter.

President and CEO of Voto Latino is a regular guest commentator on MSNBC. Data collected by Latinx organizations is cited as news items and discussed. Reporters reach out to Latinx organizations for comment and story sourcing. Framing of news also happens at the level of which sources are cited and quoted and which sources are not. Source framing in news texts also happens when Latinx sources are excluded from commenting on stories which feature Latinx issues.

In summary, the news media in the immediate aftermath of the 2018 midterm elections used the frames of homogenization and racialization outlined earlier in this book. The frame of denationalization was much less explicitly common. There were also some instances of counter-frames but were rare. Homogenization was typically framed as an interrelated phenomenon. Latinx voters were framed as prioritizing immigration issues and especially opposing anti-immigrant rhetoric by the President. They speculated that the harsh-anti-immigrant rhetoric from President Trump would lead them to vote against Republicans. After the election, Latinx voters were commonly framed as a rising force in U.S. politics. Congressional districts in California and Texas were flipped from Republicans to Democrats. Pundits attributed this shift to the increase (or even influx, as some said) of Latinx voters. This kind of framing constructs Latinx identity as essentially homogenous—Latinx voters are solely focused on one issue and vote based on immigration. Denationalizing rhetoric was much less common. I attribute this to the media's homogenizing and racializing tendencies. These two frames make Americanizing Latinx voters much less common. Instead, Americanization is a frame employed by Latinx advocates and organization to push back against these frames. The instances of counter-denationalizing framing usually related to discussing why Latinx voters in Florida tended to be more conservative, but usually without much detail or depth.

Latinx voters were also highly racialized in the media texts published immediately following the 2018 midterm elections. This tended to occur in two general methods. They were closely associated with Black voters. The phrase "Black and Latino" voters was a common refrain in the media texts. This grouping was almost elevated to a mythical status—they were responsible to increased turnout and Democratic victories in many states. This framing is also concurrent with the association of coalitional and racialization politics within U.S. politics in the 2010s. Minorities and urbanites with college degrees are associated with Democrats, while rural and white voters are associated with Republicans. It is also instructive that after the elections, President Trump quickly dropped his fearmongering of the migrant caravan. The matrix of connections between elections, campaigns, Latinxs, and the media is used opportunistically for political gain. The second major source of racialization comes from the sources the mainstream media uses to talk about Latinx voters. They mostly are not experts in Latinx issues but usually general U.S. politics experts and pundits. The news media produced as an immediate reaction to the events of the 2018 midterm elections conformed to many of the themes of Latinx identity making previously discussed in this book. We can also expect the news media to continue to cultivate these ideas until they become widely understood.

References

Abramowitz, A. I. (2010). Transformation and polarization: The 2008 presidential election and the new American electorate. *Electoral Studies, 29*(4), 594–603. doi:10.1016/j.electstud.2010.04.006

Balz, D., & Scherer, M. (2018, November 10). Anti-Trump wave hits, but with uneven force. Retrieved October 21, 2019, from https://www.washingtonpost. com/politics/for-democrats-a-midterm-election-that-keeps-on-giving/ 2018/11/09/b4075ef2-e456-11e8-ab2c-b31dcd53ca6b_story.html

Beltran, C. (2010). *The trouble with unity: Latino politics and the creation of identity.* Oxford, UK: Oxford University Press.

Bonilla-Silva, E. (2010). *Racism without racists: Color-blind racism and the persistence of racial inequality in the United States.* Lanham, MD: Rowman & Littlefield.

Bowden, J. (2018, November 06). Top trending election day search on Google: 'Dónde VOTAR'—'where to vote' in Spanish. Retrieved October 21, 2019, from https://thehill.com/policy/technology/415127-top-trending-search-on-google-for-election-day-is-donde-votar-where-to-vote

Chavez, L. R. (2013). *The Latino threat: Constructing immigrants, citizens, and the nation.* Stanford, CA: Stanford University Press.

Hardball with Chris Matthews [Transcript, Television series episode]. (2018, November 6). In *Hardball with Chris Matthews.* New York, NY: MSNBC.

Hughes, T. (2018, November 7). Dodge City showdown on voter access— Polling place transfer provokes protests. *USA Today.* Retrieved from https:// www.usatoday.com/story/news/politics/elections/2018/11/06/elections-2018-latinos-go-vote-amid-concerns-voter-suppression/1884190002/

Judis B., & Texieira, R. A. (2002). *The emerging democratic majority.* New York, NY: Scribner.

Mair, L. (2018, November 09). Don't look now, but the Mountain West is turning blue. Retrieved October 21, 2019, from https://www.thedailybeast.com/ dont-look-now-but-the-mountain-west-is-turning-blue

Newkirk (2018a, November 07). The Georgia governor's race has brought voter suppression into full view. Retrieved October 21, 2019, from https:// www.theatlantic.com/politics/archive/2018/11/how-voter-suppression-actually-works/575035/

Newkirk (2018b, November 14). Did minority voters dethrone Scott Walker? Retrieved October 21, 2019, from https://www.theatlantic.com/politics/archive/2018/11/black-and-latino-turnout-helped-defeat-scott-walker/575818/

Opinion | The School Choice Election Bonus. (2018, November 14). Retrieved October 21, 2019, from https://www.wsj.com/articles/the-school-choice-election-bonus-1542153815

Politics Nation [Television series episode]. (2018, November 17). In *Politics Nation*. New York, NY: MSNBC.

Przybyla, H. (2018, September 06). Family separations at the border help fuel new LATINO voter drive. Retrieved October 21, 2019, from https://www.nbcnews.com/politics/elections/family-separations-border-help-fuel-new-latino-voter-drive-n906906

The Role of the Latino Vote in Nevada's Senate Race. (2018, November 11). Retrieved October 21, 2019, from https://www.npr.org/2018/11/11/666646396/the-role-of-the-latino-vote-in-nevadas-senate-race

Schatz, B. (2018, November 07). A Democrat just snagged the seat Darrell ISSA held for almost two decades. Retrieved October 21, 2019, from https://www.motherjones.com/politics/2018/11/mike-levin-diane-harkey-election-results/

Steinhauer, J., & Dias, E. (2018, November 13). Arizona election results: 6 key takeaways on SINEMA Victory. Retrieved October 21, 2019, from https://www.nytimes.com/2018/11/13/us/politics/arizona-election-kyrsten-sinema.html

Trump, J. (Narrator). (2019, September). *Campaign rally*. Live performance in Santa Ana Star Center, Rio Rancho, NM.

Vargas, T. (2018, November 07). Perspective|he is Muslim and an immigrant. Does he regret voting for Trump, or will he do it again? Retrieved October 21, 2019, from https://www.washingtonpost.com/local/he-is-muslim-and-an-immigrant-does-he-regret-voting-for-trump-or-will-he-do-it-again/2018/11/07/3cede140-e29b-11e8-b759-3d88a5ce9e19_story.html

Wilcox-Archuleta, B., Gutierrez, A., Baretto, M., Diaz, S., & Oaxaca, A. (2018, November 19). *2018 midterm elections & the Latino vote* (Rep.). Retrieved October 21, 2019, from UCLA Latino Politics and Policy Initiative website: https://latino.ucla.edu/wp-content/uploads/2018/11/UCLA-LPPI-6-State-2018-Midterm-Election-Report_V3.pdf

8 Conclusion

One of the most serious controversies of 2018 related to Latinxs proved to be the separation of immigrant families from Central America seeking asylum in the United States. They were seeking refuge from the horrors of gang violence and social breakdown, which can be blamed partly on U.S. interventions throughout the 20th century. In early 2018, the Trump administration decided to institute a zero-tolerance policy for undocumented crossings. The penalty for such included the separating of children from their parents as a deterrent. Images and audio emerging from the detention centers quickly captured the attention, and incurred the anger, of the public.

Latinx advocacy groups then showed their organizing power and ability to shape the narrative. Congressional Hispanic Caucus (CHC) members started to show up at detention centers in the early days of the controversy, demanding to enter and capturing the initial media attention. Institutional Latino leaders in D.C. pressured Republican members of Congress to oppose the administration's policy. Voto Latino, partnering with other grassroots organizations, organized a series of protests at the detention facilities on the border. These rallies brought intense media scrutiny and public pressure, ultimately resulting in some backtracking by the administration, although not to the satisfaction of the aforementioned groups. While the controversy passed, the issue at hand—immigration and family separation—remained throughout 2018. According to polling, immigration was one of the major issues voters considered in the 2018 midterm elections for Republican voters.

It remains to be seen whether the family separation controversy, along with the events I focused on in this book, will inspire any large mobilization of Latino voters in elections beyond 2018. The media, as discussed in the previous chapter, seems to have settled on yes as the answer. The immigration controversy of the summer also showed that there are Latinxs in the Southwest who are more conservative and supportive of Trumpism than one would expect. In areas on the border with fewer job opportunities, the lure of federal employment with Immigrations and Customs Enforcement (ICE) is powerful. Over half of the Border Patrol is Latino. This controversy revealed that not all Latinxs will be reliable Democratic voters as many hoped they would be. There exist reactionary and conservative ideologies among Latinxs on the border. Democratic representatives on the border are involved here too. Rep. Henry Cuellar of Laredo, a CHC member, received more than $30,000 in campaign contributions from the GEO Group and its employees in 2018, according to OpenSecrets.org. The GEO Group is a company that operates private prisons and detention centers. These are among the places where families were being detained and separated.

Based on my conversations with people associated with the organizations I studied in this book, there is a growing appreciation for the ideological difference among Latinxs. The question is: is it possible to develop a Latinx political agenda removed from any ideological project? One takeaway from this study that I will expand upon later is an explanation of how the political economy of Latinx advocacy cannot be ignored when analyzing communication strategies.

The immigration controversy also sheds light on many of the other issues I have discussed in this book. I use this concluding chapter to summarize the issues discussed in this book. First, I discuss my research findings in light of the theoretical framework and scholarly research I presented in Chapters 2–4 of the book. Second, I put my research findings into conversation with the larger fields of academic literature I engaged with in this study. Here, I tease out the central contributions of my study to the field of communication, the sub-field of political communication, and the interdisciplinary approach of Latina/o/x studies. Third, as a scholar committed to developing public knowledge and as someone who tries to use accessible language in his writing, I provide several practical ways to think about Latinx political mobilization that would be useful to organizations. Fourth, I briefly discuss the limitations of my study. The limitations provoke a reflection upon the methodology typically employed in my field. Finally, I conclude by discussing the future. What future studies should naturally follow mine? And more importantly, what does the future hold for the important topic of Latinx political integration into the U.S. body politic.

Findings summarized

This book addressed the following main question: *How do U.S. Latinx advocacy organizations shape Latinx identity in the digital era of communication and the racialized public sphere of the 2010s while pursuing their goal of voter mobilization?* In Chapter 5, I addressed how organizations strategically construct an essentialistic discourse of U.S. Latinx identity. In Chapter 6, I addressed how are digital platforms used as sites of mobilizing Latinx voters, and how identity is reified and/or challenged on them. In Chapter 7, I addressed the media coverage of the Latinx vote in the 2018 midterm elections. Each chapter has sub-questions, which can be found in Chapter 1.

While the project of mobilizing actual Latinx voters over the past decade has seen mixed results, the project of developing the "new Latino" identity is well underway. The "new Latino" is a political project in that it involves an explicit call to political action—that Latinxs must show their power by voting en masse—but it is also a communication project in that it involves the creation of branded identity. The communication is constitutive, as it makes real a new demographic niche of the educated, cosmopolitan, and bilingual voting subjects. One cannot understand the political project without understanding the communication project of creating the "new Latino."

Increases in Latinx civic participation have been mixed over the past decade. There has been a general increase in the visibility of Latinx protest around immigration issues. At the same time, voting mobilization is more complex than one issue. Democratic Party officials hoped that the inciting rhetoric of Donald Trump would drive Latinxs to the polls in 2016. Clinton received slightly less of the Latinx votes than Obama did in 2012. Overall turnout of Latinx voters also decreased slightly (by .4 points) between 2012 and 2016, although Latinx voters as a share of the entire electorate increased by 1 point (Krogstad, Lopez, 2016). This seeming paradox is solved by factoring in the growth of eligible Latinx voters. Simply put, there are a lot of young Latinx people and more turn 18 every year. Civic organizations struggle to keep up with registering them. This, more than anything else, explains the persistent struggle to mobilize Latinx voters. This situation allows for a group like Voto Latino to both celebrate their record voter registrations and push new initiatives to mobilize voters. And as discussed in Chapter 5, Latinx organizations often conceptualize their mobilization targets as people who have backgrounds similar to their own, which tend to be elite. It is no mistake that Voto

Latino is now focusing on developing college chapters of the organization to mobilize new Latinx voters.

The mobilization efforts should be understood in light of recent innovations in digital campaigning. In Chapter 3, I discussed how political campaigns have rapidly adopted new technologies and strategies. As authors like Kreiss (2016) and Karpf (2012, 2016) have noted, new relations have arisen around the new digital tools available in political campaigning and advocacy organizing. I found that while Latinx organizations have a desire to use cutting-edge techniques with data from online sources to make their messages more sophisticated, they often lack the capacity to do so. Most organizational talent during this period came from political organizing, so their technical skills were less developed. And after the 2016 election, there was even a hesitancy to rely on digital organizing in an era of fake news and foreign electoral disruption. Instead, a turn toward on-the-ground organizing has been favored.

Nevertheless, communication messages online created by the organizations I studied largely conformed to what literature would suggest. Some platforms, like social media, are more conducive to engagement-based messaging, such as asking a user to sign a petition or donate. Other platforms, like email, are used simply to report information. This is similar to what Hestres (2015) found in his study of environmental advocacy groups. What is significant in my study is finding that organizational history mattered beyond platform choice. New groups were more likely to use engagement-based messaging regardless of platform, while older organizations did the opposite.

What about the communication project? Organizations that advocate on behalf of Latinx people, in coordination with corporate partners, have been successful in developing a prototype[1] of the ideal U.S. Latinx person. Marketers have called this prototype the "new Latino" (Chavez, 2013). The "new Latino" is bilingual, highly educated, cosmopolitan, and, most importantly, a sophisticated American consumer. Thus, the processes of homogenization, denationalization, and racialization all work in tandem to turn disparate populations into a discrete branded identity. Digital platforms and new media play a powerful role too. While the mass media could be critiqued as an external imposition upon Latinxs, the use of new media by trusted community actors legitimizes the socialization in American norms. The gradual corporatization of Latinx advocacy that began in the 1980s has thus transformed community mobilization into community branding. This is very much in line with what Norris called "post-modern" politics.

Perhaps the turn to community branding of U.S. Latinx people is driven by a real desire to counter the racist rhetoric of the right. If the president came to power by calling Mexican immigrants rapists and criminals, it makes some sense for Latinx advocacy organizations to portray Latinx people as hardworking, successful, educated, civically engaged, patriotic, and so on. This well-intentioned turn is emblematic of the professional and class orientation of the people who do Latinx advocacy work in the 2010s. Their background is hugely influential in the work they do in three main ways. First, they use their social networks as a resource for acquiring knowledge approximations of their audience. Thus, the people they follow online (typically people from their own class identity and professional disposition) inform their communication strategy. Second, advocates project their own experiences onto the audiences they serve. So, experiences unique to a particular class identity are universalized to all Latinxs in the United States. Finally, their class identity and professional disposition interact with the corporatization of Latinx advocacy to limit the policy proposals presented as beneficial. For example, they advocate for financial literacy instead of financial industry reform. The onus for consumer protection is placed on the consumer rather than the industry.

The theoretical model discussed in Chapter 2 very much predicted these findings, including the homogenization and Americanization of U.S. Latinxs. Dávila's (2012) and Beltran's (2010) central claim, that elite Latinxs exert a heavy influence of the construction of identity in advertising, marketing, and politics, was reinforced. This seems to suggest a twist on agenda setting, except in this case, elite Latinx actors are shaping the discourse. Rodriguez also discussed the powerful role that Spanish-language news media played in integrating Latinx people into the everyday goings-on of the nation (1999). In this forum, they were simultaneously integrated as both domestic and foreign. The communications produced by the organizations I studied tended to focus on the American features of Latinxs. DREAMers were held up as "American in all but documentation." Domestication was focused on more, possibly in response to the symbolic construction of foreignness presented by the reactionary right. At the same time, the racialization of Latinxs seemed less clear and less present. Organizations discussed the power of people of color coalitions, but there were also challenges to the construction of a singular Latinx racial identity.

The problems of framing, as typified by Scheufele (1999), can also shed some light here. Scheufele noted that the media and individuals apply framing to news events. This book has studied the framing attempts by elite Latinx actors and organizations. But what if those elite frames are mismatched with audience frames? Remember that most Latinx people choose not to use pan-ethnic labels to identify themselves. This may explain the persistent struggle to mobilize a mass of voters, the audiences being spoken to simply does not perceive they are being addressed. As seen in Chapter 7, these frames are highly aligned with media framing of Latinx voters.

Contributions summarized

The findings of this book contribute to Latina/o/x Communication Studies[2] in addition to the sub-field of political communication. First, for scholars of communication, this book makes an important intervention in detailing the political economy of ethnic and racial advocacy communication production. The class and technical expertise backgrounds of organizational actors should not be overlooked in research. Second, for scholars of both fields, this book shows how the choice to use a specific communication platform has a specific organizational context. In this case, institutional history, resources, funding (and funding reporting) mechanisms, and human talent all play important roles. In the following paragraphs, I will discuss each contribution in further detail.

Most studies of advocacy or political communication online have focused on mainstream or issue-based communication. The power of white supremacy is that certain political issues, many of which are specifically the interest of professional-class white people, are non-racialized and thus viewed as normal. An example of these issues includes taxes on wealth passed from generation to generation. However, issues like police brutality and immigration are immediately racialized. This study intervenes in this divide.

For scholars of communication studies, this study should show the importance of applying a critical political economy perspective to the knowledge being produced by Latinx organizations. It is not as simple to categorize ethnic communication as always marginal in relation to more dominant institutions. Instead, more complexity is needed. Power flows through Latinx organizations as well, especially corporate and elite domination.

The backgrounds and identities of individual actors also shape organizational choices. Organizational culture and history, in turn, shape individual choices when it comes to communication strategy. In the case of this book, all these factors collude to determine which communication platforms are prioritized over others. For example, organizations that existed in the pre-digital era and adapted to new trends in communication still tend to favor unidirectional (one to many) forms of communication, such as email. Newer groups tend to favor new media, which allows for multidirectional (many to many) conversations. Content is also influenced in a similar vein: older organizations favor reporting information, while newer groups tend to share feelings and/ or collect information.

For Latinx scholars, it is vital to consider the current communication environment as well as future iterations. It is important to recognize a point I raised early in this work—the tendency of the Internet is to simultaneously retrench and challenge identity formation. Platform and content decisions in online media also interact with the corporatization of Latinx advocacy. New platforms, such as Twitter, provide easy-to-report statistics, such as new followers and retweets, which can be used to approximate engagement for funding reports. The backgrounds of communication producers interact here as well. One result of the 2016 election was the influx of Clinton campaign talent into Latinx advocacy groups. They brought a skillset developed from political organizing that focused on using digital tools to mobilize voters, such as text reminders, voting apps, new media, and personalized email blasts. Some were used more effectively than others. The important takeaway for other scholars is to uncover how organizational choices around communication strategies (or rhetoric about Latinxs for Latinx studies scholars) are driven by history, funding resources, and human capital (i.e., where people have worked before and their skills).

Limitations of the study

Reflecting upon the research design of this study, I wondered how I could have done things differently. I worried the most about two main limitations: issues within the sample of digital communications I collected, and the limits of qualitative methodology related to researcher standpoint. In the following section, I will discuss each limitation in regard to the design, the applications to practice, and the utility of the results.

Early in the research design phase, I made the choice to collect digital communication artifacts from the organizations I studied in this book. I ended up focusing my analysis on tweets, press releases, and email blasts. There are a few issues here. First, by choosing to focus solely on communications produced by an organization, I was also choosing to ignore other communication related to the topic not directly produced by the group. For example, I could have missed a tweet related to the topic of Latinx political mobilization made by a staff member on his or her personal account. Other rich conversations also happen in replies and comments on social media. This is a consistent challenge when studying communication online—there is simply too much out there. Choosing to focus on one kind means ignoring others. This limitation does not constrain my findings, since I explicitly focused on organizations in my research question. A broader study would have to account for non-organizational communication and use a broader and more sophisticated mechanical collection method.

Nevertheless, the research method of analyzing the backgrounds of those who produce the media is a useful contribution for other scholars. Interviews, combined with supplemental data from places like LinkedIn, can create a compelling narrative about how the identities of communication producers influence the products they make. Using human- and computer-mediated communication sources focuses on the communication environment rather than on just one element.

Second, I also chose to concentrate on specific news events to focus my analysis. Two of the three news events were directly related to immigration. Here, I reinforced one of my own critiques of Latinx political communication: that it overly focuses on immigration as a Latinx issue. This selection also has an issue similar to the first limitation: that there is a chance to miss other important details. Indeed, sometimes the most interesting details can be found on the mundane days, when the news is not in crisis mode, as rare as that may have felt in 2017 and 2018. This is a more significant limitation for my results. In an ideal research environment, a longer time frame to collect data (perhaps three years instead of one) could enrich my findings.

Qualitative researchers also face issues I confronted in my research process. First, choosing to conduct interviews before analyzing digital communications influenced how I approached my analysis of the digital texts. The opposite case could also have been true if I had done the analysis of the digital texts first. My interview questions (and especially the follow-ups) may have changed. One of the key questions I asked in the expert interviews was who they think their audience is and how they learn about them. When it came time to look at email communications, the answers provided by the interviewees very much influenced the reporting/engagement division I conceptualized in Chapter 5.

Second, my own intellectual and personal history influenced how I analyzed this social phenomenon. I personally identify as Mexican American and Latino. My journey to identifying with these terms began organically while I was growing up on the border. I later intellectualized and absorbed many of the discursive frameworks of U.S. Latinx identity in college. During my graduate study, I was exposed to the field of Latina/o/x studies. I began to critically examine the construction of identity I so eagerly adopted in my younger days. Over the past few years, my political ideology has also become increasingly more left. In qualitative research, the researcher does the analysis. No matter how systematic the research is, the researcher's own biases always play a role.

By the end of 2019, the controversies of the Trump administration seemed to multiply by the day. Feelings of rage, helplessness, cynicism, and every emotion in between were common for me. A sense of fatigue set in as one crisis led to another. One of the challenges of writing this book was the constantly changing political (and emotional) terrain. Some days I felt so caught up in the news that writing felt secondary. Other days I was so emotionally exhausted from watching the news that I could not find the energy to think about my book. An issue or controversy involving Latinxs emerges weekly. I absorb and reflect on the impact it has for my research and by then another outrage has occurred. I return to my writing and see issues in new ways, attempting to capture my thoughts on a constantly shifting and amorphous topic as the news changes daily. I have discussed my own history to lay bare the potential biases that I bring forth in my analysis.

Recommendations

In theory, advocacy groups—or public interest groups, as political scientist Jeffery M. Berry calls them in his book *Lobbying for the People* (1977)—play an important role in a democracy. They represent public needs at the highest levels of government, turning public wants into policy recommendations. Writing in the 1970s, Berry categorized public interest groups as one of the many ways citizens can be involved in democracy (5). We should expect advocacy groups arise organically from the public. For example, long before LULAC was headquartered in Washington D.C., it expanded its membership in Texas before World War II.

A major problem arises if we think about the current political landscape. Theorizing advocacy groups as having an impact on policymaking is actually a stretch. We simply live in a time of elite domination. In a landmark study, political scientists Gilens and Page (2014) found that among the four groups theorized to play a role in democracy— the public, economic elites, public interest groups, and industry interest groups—the public and public interest groups played almost no role in policy- and lawmaking. In other words, policymaking is controlled entirely by economic elites and private interests.[3] Wolin (2003) has called this form of government "inverted totalitarianism." According to Wolin, actual participatory democracy no longer exists in the United States—oligarchs have completely captured the apparatus of governance. The politics that we see and participate in are simply what Wolin calls a "managed democracy," a spectacle of democracy rather than a real exercise. He writes, "Managed democracy is the application of managerial skill to the basic democratic political institution of popular elections" (140). The professionalization of politics—consultants, spin doctors, etc.—affects not just Latinx organizations (as Ortiz (1997) showed) but our democracy. At the moment, it seems that most national Latinx organizations are captured by elite interests as well. I discussed in Chapter 5 how the range of political demands by official Latinx groups is incremental and narrow, focusing on small change. More radical demands, such as the abolition of ICE, are outside the acceptable range of debate. This is managed democracy.

There are two challenges for a democracy in terms of advocacy groups. First, are they truly acting in the public interest or simply giving cover for elite interests? Here, funding structures that depend on giving from external entities matter a lot. Money is influence. Second, if groups are truly acting in the public interest, how do we deal with the possibility that these groups have little to no influence on the system? There are quite serious challenges no doubt.

So, what is to be done?

First and foremost, Latinx advocacy groups need to ditch corporate money and influence. There are two main reasons. On the broader level, continuing to rely on corporate funding (even funneled through groups like the Ford Foundation) will further entrench economic elites in the apparatus of politics. My work found a heavy corporate presence at various levels of Latinx advocacy, from sponsored tables at galas to conference panel sponsorship. Second, failing to do so in the near future will likely result in constituent backlash. There is a growing sentiment among the left that corporate money is a plague upon our houses. In 2016, Bernie Sanders captured this sentiment to run a surprisingly competitive campaign in the Democratic primary against Clinton. Others, like Alexandria Ocasio-Cortez, have won primaries against well-established Democrats. In a practical sense, Latinx advocacy groups need to abandon elite influence to remain relevant among their constituency base in the near future as millennials and members of Gen Z come of political age.

Second, there are models of organizational sustainability out there. I will highlight two potential models. First, there is the model many left organizations are adopting. Instead of focusing on large donations or sponsorships, there is a return to the old membership-based model using the infrastructure of the Internet to lower operational costs. Karpf (2012) described MoveOn.org as an early innovator in this regard. MoveOn and other recent groups, like Our Revolution, founded by staffers from the Bernie Sanders campaign, report any contribution over $5,000 on their website (Gaudiano, 2016). Most organizational revenue comes from small donor contributions.

The other model involves creating participatory experiences or programs for community members. Participants in this model have to both view attending the program as beneficial for themselves and pay (or fundraise to pay) their own way. The major benefit of this system is that those who are served by the group are also the primary investors. The downside is that this kind of model requires a shifting in organizational focus and mission. This funding model does not depend on corporate funding; most of their income comes from the program tuition participants pay. This model also has the benefit of moving organization and mobilization to the grassroots level. The combination of this model with the aforementioned model could be a new way of mobilizing Latinxs.

Third, the discussion of funding structures ultimately calls into question the overarching purpose of U.S. Latinx advocacy groups. Despite my grouping of the organizations I discussed in this book, they all have subtle differences in their missions. UnidosUS and LULAC have broad mission statements—generally to advance the well-being of Latinxs in the United States. NALEO organizes Latinx elected officials. The CHC does the same for Latinx members of Congress. Voto Latino's mission is to mobilize young Latinx voters. The Congressional Hispanic Caucus Institute (CHCI) focuses on developing young Latinx leaders. The challenge for all of these groups is to clarify what their mission means. For broadly defined missions, like those of UnidosUS and LULAC, it is deciding how much to value (and budget for) voter mobilization projects. For more narrowly oriented groups, clarifying the mission means deciding if voter mobilization should be within their portfolio (this is the case for NALEO, CHC, and CHCI especially). This was quite evident in the interviews I conducted. Staffers and decision makers were often doing the jobs of several people. Even a group like Voto Latino still focuses on some traditional advocacy, such as issuing press releases and congressional advocacy. Broad portfolios pull organizations in many different directions.

Finally, for groups explicitly oriented toward voter mobilization, my final recommendation is to reflect on the implications for U.S. Latinx identity their work produces as a side effect. Family separation at the border highlights this issue. A feature of DREAMers being framed as "Americans in all but paperwork" is the idea that they were brought into the country by no fault of their own. According to this logic, their parents made that decision for them. The casting of parents as the ones at fault proved to be a convenient frame for those trying to justify the zero tolerance policy and family separation.

More broadly, there needs to be a conversation on the utility of Latinx identity construction when so much of it is cast in reaction to external forces. This will no doubt be difficult. In its early history, LULAC did not allow non-citizens to join. Their goal was to prove the American-ness of Latinx people in the early 20th century. This desire to prove oneself to others only leads to guilt. Instead, the words of Gloria Anzaldúa should be heeded:

> You don't build bridges to safe and familiar territories, you have to risk making *un mundo nuevo*, you have to risk uncertainty of change. And *nepantla* is the only space change happens. Change requires more than words on a page—it takes perseverance, creative ingenuity and acts of love.
>
> (Anzaldúa, 1987)

Nepantla describes the place where the assumptions of U.S. Latinx identity need to be interrogated. Primarily, three assumptions need to be challenged. First is the assumption that Latinx identity can be limited to the United States. It should be possible to imagine transnational notions of common cause. This also has the side benefit of dismissing the most limiting word used to describe Latinx people: *minority*. Second, we have to be wary of the power of whiteness. White supremacy is flexible and will surely attempt to incorporate elite Latinx people, as Bonilla predicted. Finally, our rhetorical framing of Latinx people needs to banish reactive language. For example, it is certainly possible that Latinx people are in more labor-intensive jobs. But the constant framing of Latinxs as hardworking is not really about their work life. It is used to push back against reactionary right-wingers. The idea of *nepantla* calls us to move beyond this paradigm. As Anzaldúa profoundly says in *Borderlands*:

> But it is not enough to stand on the opposite river bank, shouting questions, challenging patriarchal, white conventions ... At some point, on our way to a new consciousness, we will have to leave

the opposite river bank ... Or perhaps we will decide to disengage
from the dominant culture, write it off altogether as a lost cause,
and cross the border into a wholly new and separate territory. Or
we might go another route. The possibilities are endless once we
decide to act and not react.

Anzaldúa is describing the struggle many Latinxs have. It is the pull
between mainstream white American culture and our own lived experiences. Perhaps a new pathway forward is needed.

Future directions

The construction of U.S. Latinx identity is an ongoing project. Such
a phenomenon calls for a multidimensional research agenda. In relation to political communication, much more research needs to be
done on the role of Latinx political elites. Next, as Latinx identity is
constructed by many other actors using a variety of legacy and new
media, there needs to be a focus on other spaces outside of formal politics. Finally, throughout my study and interactions, I had a persistent
thought: how do actual Latinx people think about their identities?

Latinx political elites might seem like a somewhat new social phenomenon. The discourse around Latinx politics is that Latinxs are un-
engaged and disconnected. As this study has shown, there is a small,
interconnected group of professional elites. The classic 1956 book *The
Power Elite* by sociologist C. Wright Mills shows how a small group
of tightly connected government, economic, and military elites make
most of the decisions. They often are not aware of their status as elites
(it is not a conspiracy theory), but they do internalize their role as decision makers. This book is a beginning peek into the Latinx power elite
in the United States. Much more needs to be done. Latinx leaders are
slowly moving up the ranks of the same spaces Mills discussed—the
political, economic, and military elite. Investigating the assumptions
they internalize, about Latinxs, of course, but power as well, will be
paramount.

In practical terms, what does this mean? The CHCI is focused on developing future leaders of the Latinx community in the United States.
What are the discourses about power being internalized by the young
participants? To what extent does corporate influence shape these discourses? Are there generational differences? There will also be other
ripe areas for research once young Latinxs begin to occupy positions
of power in the various spaces of life. How do they conceptualize their
positions or responsibilities?

As I discussed in the book, U.S. Latinx identity also happens in networked communication. Here, new media plays an important role. Often, the shaping of identity is being done by Latinx creators and Latinx branded platforms. I referenced brands like *We are mitú*, *Flama*, and *Remezcla* in my introduction. These brands are different than the traditional mass media producers we associate with Latinx stereotype making, like TV and advertising. The ever-increasing amount of digital media content is ripe for investigation. What does Latinx identity construction look like with influencers on social media? How is streaming music used by brands to shape identity on Spotify or Instagram?

The subjects of this socialization project, actual Latinx people themselves, also deserve attention. Without a doubt, the current moment is confusing for many. Beyond Trump, we are in the midst of a great transition from the roles and relationships of modernity (patriarchalism, strict gender roles, racial divisions, etc.) to something else. For many, this period of transition is quite uncomfortable since clear life scripts are either not available due to economic forces (the father provider script) or have fallen out of cultural favor (the white savior script). The postmodern critiques of modernity, while incredibly useful, cannot provide a new pathway for people to form new understandings of identity. Research in this moment of transition on actual Latinx people, from all sectors of life, may provide a way forward. In the end, Anzaldúa's words ring every more presciently: we are called to shape a new identity, a new way of being, and a new sense of *Latinidad* in this uncertain transition.

Notes

1 I use *prototype* here as Fehr (1993) did, meaning the knowledge structure that defines an ideal example of a category. In this case, the "new Latino" is a prototype for Latinx people in the United States.
2 Here, I use the specific name of the division of the National Communication Association.
3 This is a nicer way to say the capitalist class. I will stick to this term for now.

References

Anzaldúa, G. (1987). *Borderlands/La frontera: The new mestiza*. San Francisco, CA: Aunt Lute Books.
Beltran, C. (2010). *The trouble with unity: Latino politics and the creation of identity*. Oxford, UK: Oxford University Press.

Berry, J. M. (1977). *Lobbying for the people.* Princeton, NJ: Princeton University Press.

Chavez, C. A. (2013). Building a "new Latino" in the post-network era: Mun2 and the reconfiguration of the U.S. Latino audience. *International Journal of Communication, 7,* 1026–1045.

Dávila, A. M. (2012). *Latinos, Inc: The marketing and making of a people.* Berkeley, CA: University of California Press.

Fehr, B. (1993). How do I love thee? Let me consult my prototype. *Individuals in Relationships, 1,* 87–120. doi:10.4135/9781483326283.n4

Gaudiano, N. (2016, September 07). Bernie Sanders spinoff group to disclose big donors. Retrieved November 24, 2018, from https://www.usatoday.com/story/news/politics/onpolitics/2016/09/07/bernie-sanders-spinoff-group-disclose-big-donors/89974756/

Gilens, M., & Page, B. I. (2014). Testing theories of American politics: Elites, interest groups, and average citizens. *Perspectives on Politics, 12*(03), 564–581. doi:10.1017/s1537592714001595

Hestres, L. E. (2015). Climate change advocacy online: Theories of change, target audiences, and online strategy. *Environmental Politics, 24*(2), 193–211. doi:10.1080/09644016.2015.992600

Karpf, D. (2012). *The MoveOn effect: The unexpected transformation of American political advocacy.* Oxford, UK: Oxford University Press.

Karpf, D. (2016). *Analytic activism: Digital listening and the new political strategy.* Oxford, UK: Oxford University Press.

Kreiss, D. (2016). *Prototype politics: Technology-intense campaigning and the data of democracy.* Oxford, UK: Oxford University Press.

Krogstad, J., & Lopez, M. (2016, November 29). Hillary Clinton won Latino vote but fell below 2012 support for Obama. Retrieved October 23, 2019, from https://www.pewresearch.org/fact-tank/2016/11/29/hillary-clinton-wins-latino-vote-but-falls-below-2012-support-for-obama/

Mills, W. C. (1956). *The power elite.* New York, NY: Oxford University Press.

Ortiz, I. D. (1997). Chicana/o organizational politics in the era of retrenchment. In D. R. Maciel (Ed.), *Chicanas/Chicanos at the crossroads: Social, economic, and political change* (pp. 118–120). Tucson, AZ: University of Arizona Press.

Rodriguez, A. (1999). *Making Latino news: Race, language, class.* Thousand Oaks, CA: Sage.

Scheufele, D. (1999). Framing as a theory of media effects. *Journal of Communication, 49*(1), 103–122. doi:10.1093/joc/49.1.103

Wolin, S. S. (2003). *Democracy incorporated managed democracy and the specter of inverted totalitarianism.* Princeton, NJ: Princeton University Press.

Index

Note: **Bold** page numbers refer to tables and page numbers followed by "n" denote endnotes.

Abbott, G. 92
Abramowitz, A.I. 58
Abreu, R. 46
Acuña, R. 18
advocacy groups 56
Affordable Care Act 63
Afro-Latinxs 75–76
American Dream 67
Americanization 38, 113
"Americans of Mexican extraction" 5
Analytic Activism (2016) 56
Anderson, B. 21
Andrés, J. 80
Anguiano, C.A. 45
anti-immigrant governorship 92
Anzaldúa, G. 120–122
Aparicio, F.R. 23
Arab Spring 50
Arias, S. 39
assimilation era 36, 70
Aztlán 28

Bacon's Rebellion 20
Barnard, L. 53
Barreto, M.A. 92
Battleground Texas 92
Bayless, R. 80
Beltrán, C. 17, 26, 29, 88, 99, 113
Bernard, H. 11
Berry, J.M. 117
bespoke identities 57
Black Lives Matter movement 4, 50

"Blacks and Latinos" 103–104, 106
Blesdstein, B.J. 66
Bonilla-Silva, E. 76
Botan, C.H. 11
Bourdain, A. 80
brands, in politics 60
Brugess, J. 10
Bruns, A. 10

campaigns 52–54
Castro, J. 64, 91
Chadwick, A. 59
Charter Communications 72
Chavez, C. 28, 40, 44, 75, 104
Chester, J. 58
Chicano movement 26, 28
childhood obesity 88
Cisneros, J. 44
civic participation 111
Civil Rights Act 66, 90
classic communication theory of agenda setting 68
class identity 23–24
Clinton, H. 1, 45, 60, 64, 66, 86, 91, 111, 115, 118
collective black 76
Comcast 23, 46
Comcast NBCUniversal 72
commodification 24, 37
Communication Studies 114–115
computer-mediated communication 8, 35, 116

Congressional Hispanic Caucus
(CHC) 9, 26–27, 109, 119
Congressional Hispanic Caucus
Institute (CHCI) 119, 121
controlled interactivity 54, 85
Cooper, W.J. 20
corporate money and influence 118
corporations and commercial
interests 2, 72
Correa, T. 21
Coulter, A. 79
counter-denationalization
102–103, 106
credentialism 66
Cruz, T. 98
Cuban immigrants 36
Cuellar, H. 110
cultural similarities 22
The Culture of Professionalism
(1976) 66

DACA *see* Deferred Action for
Childhood Arrivals (DACA)
Dahlgren, P. 50, 51, 54
Dame-Griff, E.C. 88
data-based political advertising 53
data collection 8–9
Davidsen, C. 53
Dávila, A.M. 8, 17, 23, 24, 29, 30, 36,
69, 113
Day Without Immigrants 79–80
Dean campaign 56
Dean, H. 56
Deferred Action for Childhood
Arrivals (DACA) 5, 6, 8, 11, 13,
14n1, 83; advocacy organizations
88–89; DACA recipients 87–88;
denationalization 87, 88;
economic subjects 88; ideological
fissures 89; neoliberalism 88;
organizational rhetoric 90;
racialization 89; rhetorical
framing 88, 90; sleeping giant
narrative 88–89; strategic goals
87; Trump 87
De Genova, Nicholas 24, 31
Democratic National Committee
(DNC) 52
Democratic Party 44, 45, 52, 56, 58
Democratic representatives 109, 110

demographic category 1, 2, 99–100
denationalization 6, 8; agenda
setting 25; Americanness 69–70,
72; assimilation 70; assimilation
era 28–29; Congressional
Hispanic Caucus (CHC) 26–27;
corporations 72; counter-
denationalization 102–103;
definition 25, 69; denationalizing
frames 101–102; Dreamers
71; Florida Latinx voters 102;
fragmentation era 29; framing
71; historical differences 102;
immigration as Latinx issue 25–26;
Latinx advocacy organizations
71–72; Latinx political action
27–29, 32n1; legitimacy era
27–28; military service 70, 73; *vs.*
minimization of difference 25;
national anthem 70; National
Council of La Raza (NCLR)
26; project of unity 26; protest
era 28; renewed era of protest
29; symbolic renationalization
69; U.S. Americans 27; U.S.
imperialism 70–71; U.S. national
identity 70, 72–73
digital campaigning 112; *see also*
identity construction online
digital content 94–95
digital divide 41
digital-first Latinx groups 4, 82
digital media 52
Digital Youth Project 42
discourse analysis 11–12
domestication 113
draconian immigration system 7
Dream Act 83, 91
Dreamers 71, 83, 90
DREAMers 120

economic elites and industry interest
groups 118
economic protest 79
election 2016 44
engagement-based messaging 112
engagement-driven platforms 95
Entman, R.M. 16
Escobar, P. 23
Escobar, V. 93

ethnic authenticity 57
ethnography 9
exit polls 1

Facebook 49, 79
Fairclough, N. 11
family separation policy 97,
    109–110, 120
feminization 44–45
Ferrera, A. 21
Fey, T. 83
Flama 2, 122
Fordism 19
fragmentation era 29
framing/frames 16–17, 22, 88, 104,
    113–114
free expression 50, 51
Frey, L.R. 11
"Frito Bandito" 28
Fulgoni, G.M. 53
Fusion 2, 23

Garcia, S. 93
Generation Digital (Montgomery) 53
gentrification 67
Gershon, S.A. 45
get-out-the-vote (GOTV) 93
G.I. Forum 27, 28, 74
GIFs 83
Gilens, M. 117
González-Martin, R. 41
Google Trends 38
government shutdown 90
Green, D.P. 93
group consciousness 44
gubernatorial election 92

Habermas, Jurgen 50
Hardball with Chris Matthews
    (2018) 101
hashtags 50
Hatch Act 63
Hellmueller, L. 39
Herr-Stephenson, Rebecca 42
Hersh, E.D. 54, 55
Hestres, L.E. 51, 82, 112
heuristics 54
Hispandering 45
Hispanic 17
Hispanic Leadership Organization 46

homogenization 65, 113
honorary whites 76
Housing and Urban Development
    (HUD) 64
Huerta, D. 28, 45, 75
hybrid media system 4, 46, 59–60

identity: as commodity 19; as product
    57; polarization 58
identity construction online 12;
    commodification 37; mass
    electronic communication 35;
    naming 38–40; "new Latino"
    and online expression 40–43;
    representational politics 37;
    technological and media
    convergence 35–36, 47n1; U.S.
    politics as Latinx 43–47
identity politics 58–59, 94
immigration reform 1–2, 4, 24,
    109–110
Immigrations and Customs
    Enforcement (ICE) 110
indentured whites 20
informal conversational interviews 9
information-based economy 4
Internet 5–6, 35, 36, 50–51, 83, 115;
    see also political mobilization
Internet-mediated advocacy
    organizations 51
Internet of Things (IoT) 54, 61n1
"inverted totalitarianism" 118
Issenberg, S. 54

Jamieson, K.H. 52
Judis, J.B. 99

Karpf, D. 4, 13, 56, 112, 119
Katz, V. 42, 43
Kawulich, B.B. 10
Kemp, B. 103
Kennedy, J.F. 5
knowledge production 23–24
Kreiss, D. 52–53, 56, 86, 91, 112
Kreps, G.L. 11

late capitalism 19, 24, 37, 57
Latinidad 24, 76, 122
Latino 17
Latino threat narrative 44

Latinx advocacy groups 109, 113
Latinx attention and consumption 2
Latinx audience 2
Latinx identity: "Americans
  of Mexican extraction" 5;
  Deferred Action for Childhood
  Arrivals (DACA) 5, 6, 14n1;
  denationalization 6, 8; digital
  technologies 5–6; immigration
  and Latinx politics 8; Kennedy
  administration 5; media role 8;
  minimization of difference 6,
  8; NAFTA 7; pan-ethnicism 6;
  racialization 6, 8; Temporary
  Protected Status (TPS) 5, 6, 14n2;
  see also mediation of Latinx
  identity
Latinx mobilization 3
Latinx participation 1
Latinx political elites 121
Latinx population 2–3
Latinx presentation and
  representation 13; civic engagement
  86, 87; conceptualizing engagement
  85; content of messages 82, **82**;
  controlled interactivity 85; DACA
  87–89; data operations 91–92;
  Day Without Immigrants 79–80;
  Democratic Party 91; digital
  communication 80; digital content
  81, 94–95; digital tools 94–95;
  economic protest 79; email and
  press releases 83; end of funding
  90; engagement-driven platforms
  95; GIFs 83; human resources
  84; Internet culture 83; Latinos
  Vote 85; Latinx socialization
  95; modes of communication
  84; NCLR 86; *Opportunidad*
  app 85; organizational history
  82; organizational leadership
  83; platforms and messages **82**,
  82–87; shutdown 89–92; simulated
  engagement 85; social media 83;
  "standing with" Dreamers 90–91;
  technological ambivalence 86; 2018
  Texas democratic primary 92–94;
  VoterPal 84; WhatsApp 79–80;
  Women's March 79
Latinx socialization 95

League of United Latin American
  Citizens (LULAC) 3, 9, 27, 28
Lebaron, A. 24
legacy groups 51, 82
legitimacy era 27–28, 93
Let's Move! Campaign 88
Limbaugh, R. 79
limitations of study: qualitative
  methodology 116–117; sample of
  digital communications 115–116
Lipsman, A. 53
Lobbying for the People (Berry) 117
Lopez, J. 21, 23
Lozano, A. 38
LULAC 9, 68, 74, 82–84, 90, 119

McLuhan, Marshall 82
Maddow, R. 101
Maid in Manhattan 21
"managed democracy" 118
Marchi, R. 43
mass electronic communication 35
Matthews, C. 104
mediation of Latinx identity 12;
  denationalization 25–29; Fordism
  19; framing/frames 16–17; identity
  as commodity 19; late capitalism
  19; minimization of difference
  22–25; political and economic
  moment 18–19; pre-Internet
  communication technologies 31;
  racial formation theory 19–22;
  racialization 29–32; terminology
  17–18
mediatization theory 52
memorandum of understanding
  (MOU) 46
Mendez v. Westminster 29
Mercado, W. 36
Mestizaje 75
Mestizos 75
Mexican American Legal
  Defense and Educational Fund
  (MALDEF) 64
Mexican Americans 74–75, **75**
military service 70
Mills, C.W. 121
minimization of difference 6, 8;
  American Dream 67; bilingual
  television network 23; class

identity 65, 67; class identity and knowledge production 23–24; commodified culture production 24; credentialism 66; cultural similarities 22; demographic destiny 99–100; education 66; elite networks 68; ethnic elites 66, 68; generalized representations of Hispanidad 23; gentrification 67; Hispanic marketing 23–24; homogenization 65, 69, 99, **99**; hybrid media environment 69; immigration 24, 100–101; information sources 68; Latinx market 69; marketing and commercial media 25; monolithic community 68–69; nativist rhetoric 68; online media 65; passive electoral force 100; physical phenotypes 22; politics and political campaign 22; professionalism as social status 66; professional political class position 65, 66; racial and ethnic difference 25; Spanish language 22–23; Spanish-speaking market 24

MiTú 2
Mizuko Ito 42
models of organizational sustainability 119
Montgomery, K.C. 28, 53, 58
Montoya, D. 38
Mora, G.C. 17, 30, 36
Mother Jones 100
Moura, W. 23
The Move On Effect (Karpf) 4, 56
multiethnic coalition 1–2
mun2 23, 40
Murray, J. 66, 68, 72, 87
music 75, and politics 53

NAFTA 7
National Association of Latinx Elected and Appointed Officials (NALEO) 9, 74, 92, 93, 119
national conventions 9–10
National Council of La Raza (NCLR) 4, 9, 26, 84, 86
National Hispanic Leadership Agenda (NHLA) 63–64

National Honey Board 41
national identity 22
navigational capital 43
NBCUniversal (NBCU) 40, 46
negative partisanship 60
neo-liberal language 46
nepantla 120
networked Latinx identity formation 77–78
"new Latino" 2, 59–60, 111, 112; access divide 41–42; access points 42; affordances divide 42; brokering 42–43; digital divide 41; Digital Youth Project 42; Latinx youth 42–43; navigational capital 43; *quince* planners 40–41; remixing and configurability 41
Nielsen, A.E. 11, 40
No Country for Old Men 21
Nørreklit, H. 11
Norris, P. 57, 60

Obama, B. 1, 4, 53, 54, 56, 58, 60, 63, 64, 66, 74, 92, 104, 111
Obama, M. 88
Ocasio-Cortez, A. 118
Occupy Wall Street 50
Omi, M. 19, 20
online media 35
online political advertising 53–54
optimizer 53
O'Reilly, B. 79
organizational history 112, 114–115
O'Rourke, B. 98
"outsourced" innovation 52
overarching purpose of U.S. Latinx advocacy groups 119

Page, B.I. 117
Panagopoulos, C. 93
pan-ethnicism 6
participant observation 9–10
partisanship 55; negative 60
people of color (POC) 30, 74
Perez, S.L. 66, 68, 72, 87
Pero Like 2
personal brand 57
physical phenotypes 22
Pledge of Allegiance 70
Poehler, A. 83

political advertising 53–54, 60
political mobilization 12; accepted
  notion of reality 50; audience-
  identity constructions 54–56;
  campaigns 52–54; digital politics
  49–51; Facebook 49; formal
  organizations 51; free expression
  50, 51; hashtags 50; Internet
  50–51; "new Latino" hybrid 59–60;
  political advertising online 53–54;
  post-modern identity and politics
  57–59; social movement 50; "U.S.
  Liberal" 49; Web 2.0 49–50
politics: music and 53; of platforms
  81; post-modern identity
  57–59, 112
post-modernism 57
*Presidential Campaigning in the
  Internet Age* (Stromer-Galley) 85
professionalism, as social status 66
professionalization, of political
  communication 54, 118
professional political class 12–13;
  denationalization 69–73;
  minimization of difference
  65–69; networked Latinx identity
  formation 77–78; racialization
  73–77, **75**; in Trump era 64; White
  House Latinx policy summit 63–64
project of unity 26
protest era 28
public, and public interest groups
  117–118
Puerto Rican movement 3, 26
puertorriqueños 28
pundits 44, 104–106
purchasing power 21

qualitative content analysis 11
qualitative field research 9–10
quinceañera 40, 59

race, definition of 19–20
racial difference 31, 74
racial formation theory 19–22
racial inferiority 20
racialization 6, 19, 20; Afro-Latinxs
  75–76; agenda of organization
  30–31; "Blacks and Latinos"
  103–104; coalition of voters 104;

collective black 76; Dominican
  Republic 73; elite Latinxs 76–77;
  Hispanics 30; honorary whites 76;
  indigenous people 73; *Latinidad*
  76; Latinxs racial identity 29;
  mainstream media 107; Mexican
  Americans 74–75, **75**; national
  identities 31; people of color
  (POC) 30, 74; pundits 104–105;
  racial categories and politics
  73–74; racial difference 31;
  racial difference among Latinxs
  74; Spanish and Portuguese
  colonialism 73; triracial system 73
racial politics 4
Racism without Racists (Bonilla-
  Silva) 76
racist replacement theory 101
rainbow coalition principle 104
Ramos, J. 25, 26
Ramos-Zayas, Ana Yolanda 24, 31
Remezcla 122
renationalization 25, 27, 69
renewed era of protest 29
representational politics 37, 94
rhetorical framing 88, 93
Rinderle, S. 38
Rocha, R. 90
Rock the Vote 53
Rodriguez, A. 7, 17, 21, 25, 27, 29,
  30, 36
Ryan, G. 11

Saenz, T. 64
Salinas, C. 38
Sanders, B. 104, 118, 119
Scheufele, D. 16, 113
scholars of communication
  studies 114
Segura, G.M. 92
semantic web 56
semi-structured, standardized expert
  interviews 9
Shirky, C. 50
shutdown 89–92
Sicario 21
sleeping giant narrative 44, 45,
  88–89, 99
Smith, J.A. 46
social diffusion of technology 36

social imaginaries 17–18
social media 36
Soto-Vásquez, A.D. 5, 55
Southwest Voter Registration
    Education Project (SVREP) 26, 74
Spanish language 92–93; efficiency
    22–23; news 21–22
Spanish-speaking market 24
"standing with" Dreamers 90–91
State of the Hispanic Consumer 40
Stokes-Brown, A. 43, 44
Stromer-Galley, J. 54, 85
Sunstein, C.R. 50
symbolic renationalization 69

technological and media convergence
    35–36, 47n1
technology-intensive campaigning 52
Telecommunications Act of 1996 40,
    47n2
Telemundo 23, 40
Temporary Protected Status (TPS) 5,
    6, 14n2
terminology 17–18
Texas democratic primary 92–94
Texiera, R. 99
transnational flows of migration 18
Treaty of Guadalupe Hidalgo 3, 27
Tripp, Lisa 42
Trippi, J. 56
triracial system 73, 76
The Trouble with Unity (Beltrán) 26
Trump, D. 1, 11, 21, 25, 26, 44, 58, 60,
    64, 74, 79, 80, 87, 95, 97, 98, 100,
    103, 105, 106, 109, 111, 117, 122
2018 midterm election 13;
    denationalization 101–103;
    differences among Latinx voters
    101; family separation policy 97;
    Latinx story 105–107; Latinx voter
    turnout 97; media about Latinx
    voters **98**, 98–99; minimization of
    difference 99–101; news sources
    98, **98**; racialization 103–105;

Senate elections 98; sleeping giant
    narrative 99; themes of U.S. Latinx
    identity 98–99, **99**
Twitter 115

Ugly Betty 21
UnidosUS 4, 9, 26, 83, 84, 119
United We Dream 4
units of analysis 10–11
Univision 2, 23, 40
U.S. Americanness 27, 69–70
U.S. Hispanic Chamber of
    Commerce 31
U.S. Latinx advocacy groups 3–4
U.S. Latinx identity 120–121
"U.S. Liberal" 49

Valderrama, W. 70
Vallejo, J.A. 9
Vargas, T. 105
Vergara, S. 20
Vigil, M. 26
VoteBuilder 52
Voter Activation Network (VAN) 86
voter eligibility 55
VoterPal 84
Voto Latino 4, 9, 37, 68, 83, 84, 93,
    94, 109, 119

Wal-Mart 72
We are mitú 122
West Side Story
    (Negrón-Muntaner) 20
White House Latinx policy summit
    63–64
white supremacy 120
Winant, H. 19, 20
Wolin, S.S. 118
Women's March 79

Yosso, T.J. 43
Young Lords 28

zero-tolerance policy 109, 120

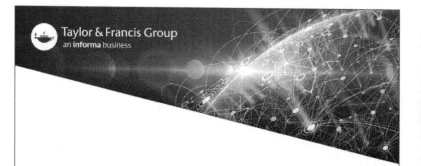

Printed in the United States
by Baker & Taylor Publisher Services